THE CASE FOR
TRADITIONAL
PROTESTANTISM

THE CASE FOR TRADITIONAL PROTESTANTISM

*The Solas of the
Reformation*

Terry L. Johnson

THE BANNER OF TRUTH TRUST

THE BANNER OF TRUTH TRUST
3 Murrayfield Road, Edinburgh EH12 6EL, UK
P O Box 621, Carlisle, PA 17013, USA

*

© Terry L. Johnson 2004
ISBN 0 85151 888 5

*

Typeset in 11/14 pt Sabon at
The Banner of Truth Trust
Edinburgh

*

Printed in Great Britain by
Bell and Bain Ltd.,
Glasgow

To the Members of the
Independent Presbyterian Church
of Savannah, georgia,
militant and triumphant,
who for 250 years
have been holding aloft
the torch of truth

CONTENTS

PREFACE

'Biblical Christianity' is what I prefer to call the understanding of the gospel which unfolds in the following pages. The Reformation sought to return to the original sources (*ad fontes*) – to the Bible and the earliest Christian writings – in order to rediscover and revive Christianity in its original and purest form. The Reformers were eager to bring the church's beliefs and practices, its worship and message, into conformity with the Bible's teaching. It was a noble vision: purge the church of its corruptions and reform it according to God's Word. Who can but admire that?

Still, we have a problem. What shall we call those who are still today inspired by the Reformers' vision? Their children were called *Protestants*. But for some that label evokes images of the awful wars of religion of the sixteenth and seventeenth-centuries, and of bitter religious bigotry in places of continuing sectarian strife today.

Evangelical might do. It was once a synonym for Protestant, and a positive one at that. Who can argue against being an evangelical, one who loves the *evangel* – the gospel, the good news of Jesus Christ? Yet today this term too has been hijacked by the bad guys. For many it evokes images of crooked Elmer Gantry on the sawdust trail, of white-shoed, slick-haired, televangelists and their endless appeals for money.

Shall we then eschew these terms in favour of *biblical Christianity*? Frankly, while biblical Christianity is what we advocate, this label seems to be presumptuous. It rather begs the question, doesn't it? Many groups claim to be biblical, after all, even cults. To call what we advocate biblical Christianity offers little in the way of clarification.

What shall we do? We are forced, for now, to rely on the old terms 'Protestant' and 'Evangelical' as shorthand for the understanding of the church and its message that we wish to promote. But we beg the reader to understand these terms in their best sense, not as corrupted by those who have betrayed the gospel, but as used by the first generation of Reformers. We share their vision of a gospel purged and purified according to the Word of God, and the church restored to its biblical and apostolic integrity.

TERRY L. JOHNSON
September 2004

I

THE EVANGELICAL FAITH

On 31 October 1517, an Augustinian monk nailed to the door of the Castle Church in Wittenberg 'Ninety-five Theses' or 'Complaints' against abuses in the church of his day. His complaints, which were actually a call for reform, were quickly copied and distributed, first throughout Germany, and then all of Europe. Unwittingly, Martin Luther (1483–1546) had started a revolution, called the Protestant Reformation, which would forever alter the face of Western Civilization, and through it, the world.

Socially, the Protestant Reformation broke down the wall between the sacred and the secular, leading to a fresh appreciation for marriage, family, and the ordinary tasks of life.

Politically, it led to the recognition of an essential equality among all people, a recognition of basic human rights, and accordingly the creation of representative forms of government.

Economically, it promoted free-market economics and gave workers a new sense of dignity in their labours.

Educationally, it gave impetus to universal literacy, as the common people learned to read the Bible for themselves.

In a word, the Reformation led to freedom: personal, political, economic, and intellectual.

The Protestant Reformation had profound effects upon all aspects of society, but its chief effects were *religious*. Luther and the Protestant Reformers brought much needed reforms to the church. Do you appreciate *congregational singing*? Then thank the Reformers for reviving it. Do you believe the *Bible* should be read in the language of the people? Then thank Martin Luther and his German Bible for paving the way for a host of new translations of the Hebrew and Greek Scriptures into the vernacular. Is your soul spiritually fed by *preaching*? Then thank the Reformers for restoring the preached Word to its central place in the life of the people of God. Do you think *communion* should be taken in 'both kinds', the bread and the wine? Then thank Martin Luther for restoring the cup to the laity. Do you believe in the *ministry of every member of the church*? Then thank the Reformers for emphasizing it.[1] Do you know the answer to the question, 'What must I do to be saved?' Then thank Martin Luther for rescuing the biblical answer to that question from the medieval innovations by which it had been obscured.

Martin Luther, Ulrich Zwingli (1484–1531), John Calvin (1509–1564), John Knox (c.1514–1572), and other Reformers endeavoured to restore the church to its apostolic purity. Their faith was called an 'evangelical faith' because, like the early church before them, they stressed the 'evangel', the gospel, the good news of Jesus Christ.

The five cries of *sola* ('alone' or 'only') which served as rallying-calls for their generation continue to be fundamental gospel principles today. They represent the core commitments of classic

---

[1] We note with thanksgiving that, since Vatican II, the Roman Catholic Church has embraced these reforms: congregational singing, vernacular services, communion in both kinds, lay ministry, lay Bible reading and study. Yet on more fundamental issues, Vatican II reaffirmed the decrees of the Council of Trent (1545–63); the sacrificial nature of the mass, justification by a combination of faith and works, the priestly nature of the clerical office, the magisterium as the final source of religious authority.

Protestantism, modern evangelicalism, and even of 'mere Christianity'. We affirm them, and now review them, not as a historical exercise, but to reaffirm the central commitments of the Christian faith. The solas help uncover the heart of the gospel, illuminating what it means to be a Christian. Scripture alone, Christ alone, faith alone, grace alone, God's glory alone; upon these five solas the Reformers stood, and upon these we continue to stand today.

Faith Alone (Sola Fide)

What must I do to be sure of life in the next world, to ensure what the Bible calls 'eternal life', life in eternity? Another way that the Bible puts this question is, what must I do to be saved, to be delivered from the guilt of my sin and reconciled to God? Martin Luther struggled with this question for more than 10 years. His pilgrimage to faith began in July 1505, at the age of 21. While caught out in a rainstorm he was nearly hit by a lightning bolt. In a flash he saw horrible visions of fiends in hell and in terror cried out, 'St Anne, help me! I will become a monk.'[2]

That week Luther entered the monastery and began there his search for the assurance of God's love and favour and a sure escape from the terrors of his wrath and hell. An earnest young man, he diligently followed the ascetic practices which the church taught were the way to please God and secure a place in heaven. He fasted. He prayed. He slept without blankets. He deprived himself of all worldly comforts and pleasures. Yet all he did seemed to fall short of securing the assurance of salvation. No matter how hard he tried, his efforts could not compensate for the weight of his guilt. He could sense only God's anger, not his love. Luther later said, 'If ever a monk got to heaven by monkery, it was I.' Yet he knew in his heart that his best efforts, his purest works, were not enough.

[2] The following quotations are taken from Bainton, *Here I Stand: A Life of Martin Luther* (New York: Abingdon-Cokesbury Press, 1950), pp. 34, 37–51.

In November 1510, Luther journeyed to Rome, the 'Holy City', where he thought he might find peace with his Maker. There he sought to appropriate the merits of the saints. The church taught that anyone could receive some of the merit that had been earned by deceased saints. This merit would make the recipient more holy in the eyes of God and ensure his passage to heaven. Luther, like many Christians of his day, sought to access this saintly merit. He viewed alleged relics, such as a twig from the burning bush and one of the coins that Judas was paid for his treachery. He attended masses and repeated the *Pater Noster* (the Lord's Prayer). He visited the holy sites. While Luther earned considerable merit from the 'treasury of the saints', he still felt no satisfaction. He felt alienated from God. After crawling on his knees up the *scala sancta* – supposed steps of Pilate's Palace – saying the *Pater Noster* on each step, he arrived at the top and said, 'Who knows whether it is so?'

In April 1511, Luther was transferred by the Augustinian order to Wittenberg, Germany. There he began to seek peace with God through the confession of sins. And confess his sins he did! Even though he was a monk, living in a monastery, a lifestyle that would offer limited opportunity for sin, one would think, he sometimes spent up to six hours a day on his knees confessing his sins, terrified that he should forget even one. No matter how hard he worked at confessing in this way, he still felt no closer to God's love or the peace of the assurance of salvation.

Realizing the futility of this approach he began to study the German Mystics. Their writings urged him to stop striving and surrender himself to the love of God. He must yield. He must surrender all of self and all assertiveness. He must 'let go and let God' (as some might say today). Luther felt he was coming closer to the answer, but not quite reaching it. The mystical approach would work for a while. He would feel himself at peace with God and with himself, but the feeling would last only for a season. Then he would crash and fall under the burden of his guilt. God's anger was too great! The distance between him and God was too far! The holy God could not be satisfied with any of his efforts. Luther despaired, 'I was myself more than once driven to the very abyss of despair so that I wished I had never been created. Love God? I hated him!'

The turning point came for Luther when he was asked to study for his doctorate and to take the Chair of Biblical Studies at the University of Wittenberg. The more he studied, the clearer the gospel became. He taught the Psalms (1513), Romans (1515), and Galatians (1516). Yet he continued to wrestle with the phrase 'the righteousness of God', which he took to mean God exacting his just retribution, his pound of flesh, a debt everyone owed and no one could escape. Finally, Luther had what has sometimes been called his 'Tower Experience' (labelled as such because it is believed to have come to him in his study in the tower of the Augustinian monastery at Wittenberg). In the course of his regular preparations to lecture, he at long last came to understand the gospel.[3] Let us pick up his own account of his conversion:

I greatly longed to understand Paul's epistle to the Romans and nothing stood in the way but that one expression, 'the righteousness of God', because I took it to mean that justice whereby God is just and deals justly in punishing the unjust. My situation was that, although an impeccable monk, I stood before God as a sinner troubled in conscience, and I had no confidence that my merit would assuage Him. Therefore I did not love a just, angry God, but rather hated and murmured against Him. Yet I clung to the dear Paul and had a great yearning to know what he meant.

Night and day I pondered until I saw the connection between the righteousness of God and the statement that 'the just shall live by faith.' Then I grasped that the righteousness of God is that righteousness by which through grace and sheer mercy God justifies us through faith. Thereupon I felt myself to be reborn and to have gone through open doors into paradise. The whole of Scripture took

---

[3] His moment of understanding has been dated as early as the Autumn of 1514 during his lectures on the Psalms, and as late as 1519 (see Bernhard Lohse, *Martin Luther's Theology: Its Historical and Systematic Discovery* [Minneapolis: Fortress Press, 1999], pp. 85ff.

on a new meaning, and whereas before 'the righteousness of God' had filled me with hate, now it became to me inexpressibly sweet in greater love. This passage of Paul became to me a gate to heaven ... If you have a true faith that Christ is your Saviour, then at once you have a gracious God, for faith leads you in and opens up God's heart and will, that you should see pure grace and should look upon His fatherly, friendly heart, in which there is no anger nor ungraciousness. He who sees God as angry does not see Him rightly but looks only on a curtain, as if a dark cloud had been drawn across his face.[4]

Luther's insight continues to be crucial for us today. What must we do to be saved? Must we complete sufficient good works? Religious works? Social works? No. What we must do is believe in the Lord Jesus Christ as our Saviour. Salvation by faith in Jesus Christ is what the Bible teaches and what we still find to be true. It is the one 'who does not work but believes' who is saved (*Rom.* 4:5). It is by *faith alone* that we are justified. It is by *faith alone* that we receive Christ's word of forgiveness and the assurance of eternal life.

What about our works? What about keeping the Ten Commandments, attending church, receiving the sacraments, being helpful to others, and doing our best? Is it not faith plus works? Do our works not contribute to our salvation? We say with Calvin, 'Assuredly we do deny that in justifying a man they are worth one single straw.'[5]

Why should God let me into heaven? Believers must continue to answer, 'Only because of what Christ has done for us on the cross which we have received, not because of any good works that we have done or that the church has done for us.' Christ is received only through empty-handed, beggarly faith. It is by faith alone apart from works that we are saved.[6]

---

[4] Bainton, *Here I Stand*, p. 65.
[5] John C. Olin (ed), *A Reformation Debate: John Calvin and Jacopo Sadoleto* (Grand Rapids: Baker Book House, 1966, 1976), p. 67.
[6] Confusion continues on this point: 'It would be . . . foolish, as well as presumptuous . . . to claim to receive forgiveness while doing without the

Christ Alone (Solo Christo)

Luther did not immediately recognize the ecclesiastical ramifications of his understanding of *sola fide*, faith alone. 'He had not yet thought through the practical implications of his theology for the theory of the church, her rites, her composition, and her relation to society', says Bainton.[7] Those practical implications were to prove profound.

Following the posting of the Ninety-five Theses, Luther engaged in various discussions and debates with church and academic leaders, including the Heidelberg Disputation in April 1518, his interview with Cardinal Cajetan in October of the same year, and his Leipzig debate with John Eck in July 1519. With the arrival of the Papal Bull ('Bull' is from the Latin *bulla*, meaning 'seal', referring to the seal affixed to an official document) in October 1520, which demanded that Luther recant or face excommunication, his life erupted in a fury of activity leading to his trial in Worms, Germany, in April 1521, described below.

But for one year, October 1519 to October 1520, he enjoyed relative calm. He used the time well. Luther wrote feverishly, producing a number of works, including the three that have been called his 'Three Great Reformation Treatises', the *Address to the German Nobility*, *The Babylonian Captivity of the Church*, and *The Freedom of the Christian Man*. In these Luther worked out the 'practical implications' of his evangelical insight: if we are justified by faith alone it must be that we look to Christ alone, not to the church, its priests, and its sacraments, for salvation.

Luther's Christ-centred theology became clear in the most radical of his writings, *The Babylonian Captivity of the Church*.[8] Church historian and theologian Philip Schaff (1819–93) spoke of it as a

---

sacrament of penance', says John Paul II (see also *Christianity Today*, September 6, 1985. The quotation is from the *Apostolic Exhortation on Reconciliation and Penance*).

[7] Bainton, p. 136.

[8] Martin Luther, 'The Babylonian Captivity of the Church', in *Three Treatises* (Philadelphia: Fortress Press, 1970).

'polemical, theological work of far-reaching consequences'. In it, he attacks the sacramental system of the Roman Church, by which she controls the life of the Christian from the cradle to the grave, and brings every important act and event under the power of the priest. This system he represents as a captivity, and Rome as the modern Babylon.[9]

Here is how the system worked. One was baptized as an infant, confirmed as a youth, married as a mature person, and received extreme unction on one's death bed. Each of these ceremonies, along with ordination, were seen as sacraments, conveying grace when administered by a priest. The grace conferred through these sacraments was supplemented throughout one's life by regular confession of sin (the sixth sacrament) to a priest and the reception of the eucharist (the seventh sacrament). From the 'cradle to the grave', as Schaff says, the Christian was dependent upon and controlled by the church if he would receive the grace by which alone he could be saved. Luther studied the Bible and church history, and saw not seven sacraments but two, reducing 'with one stroke', says Bainton, the number of sacraments by five.[10]

The effect was to shift focus from the church and its clergy as the sole administrators of grace to Christ alone. The elimination of confirmation and extreme unction (last rites) reduced the control of the church over the young and the aged. The removal of penance (confession) diminished the power of the priests as the agents through which forgiveness could be obtained. The elimination of ordination as a sacrament 'demolished the caste system of clericalism and provided a sound basis for the priesthood of all believers', notes Bainton.[11] Most important of all, Luther, for the first time, denied transubstantiation. He argued that the mass was not a sacrifice, but a supper. Though Christ is truly present, the substance of the bread and wine do not (through

[9] Philip Schaff, *History of the Christian Church, Volume II: Modern Christianity: The German Reformation* (Grand Rapids: Eerdmans Publishing Company, 1910, 1950), p. 214.
[10] Bainton, p. 137.   [11] Ibid.

the powers supposedly conferred upon priests at their ordination) become the substance of Christ's body and blood (while their 'accidents', or appearance, remain unchanged). Moreover the laity, who had been denied the cup for a thousand years, were to receive communion in both kinds, both the bread and the cup. What were believers now to do? Denied the grace of confirmation, marriage, extreme unction, penance, transubstantiated bread and wine, and the priestly powers that activate the grace that allegedly flows from them, where were they to look for grace? Luther answered: Believers should look to 'Christ alone'. Christ alone is our Saviour. Christ alone is our Sacrifice. Christ alone is our Mediator. We confess our sins to him; at death we look to him as our only hope of eternal life; at the Lord's Supper we enjoy communion or table fellowship with him (*1 Cor.* 10:15, 16). 'The cross alone is our theology', said Luther.[12] At this assault the whole Roman system came tumbling down: priesthood, mass as sacrifice, church as sole dispenser of grace. The grace that saves comes to each believer immediately from Christ through the gospel. Rome was forced by these arguments to either reform or reject the insights of the Reformation. 'The breach is now irreparable', said Erasmus, upon reading *The Babylonian Captivity of the Church*.[13]

Moreover, because the Scripture teaches the uniqueness and sufficiency of Christ's mediatorial office, Luther and the Reformers (for example, Cranmer, Calvin, Knox, Bucer) affirmed the priesthood of all believers. Each believer, they said, has the right of direct access to God in Christ. We are 'a royal priesthood' (*1 Pet.* 2:9). Christ 'has made us to be a kingdom, priests to His God and Father' (*Rev.* 1:6). Our privilege, joy and right is to go directly to God through Jesus Christ without the help of any

---

[12] Alister E. McGrath, *Luther's Theology of the Cross* (Oxford: Basil Blackwell Ltd., 1985), p. 152; also Gerhard O. Forde, *On Being a Theologian of the Cross: Reflections on Luther's Heidelberg Disputation, 1518* (Grand Rapids: Eerdmans, 1997).

[13] Bainton, p. 137.

created being.[14] He alone makes us partakers of the blessings of redemption. He alone is the Saviour. He alone is the Mediator. 'His [Luther's] was a Christological corrective', says Protestant scholar James Atkinson. 'I have taught you Christ, purely, simply, and without adulteration', Luther maintained until the end of his life.[15]

Scripture Alone (Sola Scriptura)

The medieval church put final authority in matters of faith and practice in the hands of the Pope. Conciliarism, which attempted in the fifteenth century to assert the authority of councils over the popes, had been suppressed. The Pope alone had the power authoritatively to interpret Scripture, tradition, the Church Fathers, and, for that matter, the Church Councils. He even had the power to formulate new doctrines. Luther gave decisive authority to Scripture in all matters of faith and practice. Opponents 'scarcely ever attempted to answer Luther on the basis of Scripture', as Lohse points out.[16] They appealed to the authority of the Pope, the church councils, the Fathers, and to tradition. While not depreciating these authorities, Luther came to see that final, decisive authority must rest upon Scripture alone. By July 1519, Luther was saying to John Eck during the Leipzig Disputation:

> A simple layman armed with Scripture is to be believed above a pope or a council without it. As for the pope's decretal on indulgences I say that neither the Church nor the pope can establish articles of faith. These must come from Scripture. For the sake of Scripture we should reject pope and councils.[17]

[14] In our own day Pope John Paul II has dismissed the 'widespread idea that one can obtain forgiveness directly from God' and continues to exhort the faithful to confess their sins more often to their priests (*Miami Herald*, December 12, 1984). He says 'Mary is the source of our faith and our hope', (*Christianity Today*, September 6, 1985, quoting from the *Homily at Mass at Cap de la Madeleine Shrine*).

[15] J. Atkinson, 'Luther, Martin', in *New Dictionary of Theology* (Downers Grove, Ill.: Inter-Varsity Press, 1988), pp. 403–4.

[16] Lohse, p. 188.   [17] Bainton, p. 117.

Luther's year-long repose following Leipzig was shattered in October 1520 with the arrival in Wittenberg of the Papal Bull *Exsurge Domine,* condemning Luther and his works and demanding his recantation within sixty days. Luther defiantly responded by refusing to burn his writings, burning instead the Papal Bull. 'This Bull condemns Christ Himself', he declared.[18]

The Holy Roman Emperor Charles V agreed with the church that Luther should be tried at the upcoming 'Diet', or Assembly of the German Nation, which was to meet at Worms in April 1521. There, before the Emperor and the whole assembly of German princes and representatives of the church, Luther was examined. As the trial came to its dramatic close, the Archbishop of Trier demanded that he recant.

> Martin, how can you assume that you are the only one to understand the sense of Scripture? Would you put your judgement above that of so many famous men and claim that you know more than they all? You have no right to call into question the most holy orthodox faith, instituted by Christ the perfect lawgiver, proclaimed throughout the world by the apostles, sealed by the red blood of the martyrs, confirmed by the sacred councils, defined by the Church in which all our fathers believed until death and gave to us as an inheritance, and which now we are forbidden by the pope and the emperor to discuss lest there be no end of debate.

Then finally, it was put to him, 'I ask you, Martin – answer candidly and without horns – do you or do you not repudiate your books and the errors which they contain?'

Luther, knowing that his life probably depended upon how he answered, said:

> Since then your Majesty and your lordships desire a simple reply, I will answer without horns and without teeth. Unless I am convicted by Scripture and plain reason – I do not accept the authority of popes and councils, for they have contradicted each other – my conscience is captive to the Word of God. I cannot and I will not recant

---

[18] Bainton, p. 160.

anything, for to go against conscience is neither right nor safe. Here I stand. I cannot do otherwise. God help me. Amen.[19]

We see in Luther's stand a number of Reformation principles, such as the right of private judgment and freedom of conscience. A believer has the right before God to make judgments about truth and error, and to follow his or her own conscience. But above all we see the principle of *sola Scriptura*.

Luther's words thrill the hearts of believers because we too are captives of the Word of God. We believe that God's 'infallible' Word (as Luther called it) is 'the rule of faith and practice'.[20] Scripture is the only firm ground upon which the individual believer and the church can stand.

Belief and practice in the church must not be based upon creeds or councils or clerics, not on common sense, logic, intuition, science or even new revelation. Scripture alone – the infallible, inerrant, completely sufficient written Word of God – is our only rule of faith and practice.

Grace Alone (Sola Gratia)

At the height of the Reformation conflict with Rome, the great humanist scholar Desiderius Erasmus (c.1426–1536) published his *Discussion concerning Free Will* (1524), attacking Luther and casting his lot with the Papacy. Erasmus had been sympathetic to the Reformation. He published the first printed text of the New Testament in Greek in 1516, with accompanying notes that were highly critical of Rome. It has often been said that 'Erasmus laid the egg that Luther hatched.' Erasmus had waited long (too long, according to Henry VIII and the Pope himself) to choose sides. It had been seven years since the publishing of the Ninety-five Theses. When he finally did declare himself, it was surprising that the issue was that of 'free will', rather than one of the more burning issues: the sacraments, justification, or church authority.

---

[19] The above quotations are taken from Bainton, p. 185.
[20] *Westminster Confession of Faith*, I.ii.

Instead he attacked Luther's understanding of sin's impact upon the human will.

Yet what may be surprising to us was not to Luther. 'You alone have attacked the real thing, that is, the essential issue', he told Erasmus.

> You have not worried me with those extraneous issues about the Papacy, purgatory, indulgences and such like trifles, rather than issues in respect of which almost all to date have sought my blood . . . you, and you alone, have seen the hinge on which all turns, and aimed for the vital spot. For that I heartily thank you; for it is more gratifying to me to deal with this issue.[21]

Does the human will have the capacity to believe and obey the gospel? Does a positive response to Christ require God's gracious enabling, or do sinners have this ability on their own, without help? This question is the 'hinge on which all turns', as Luther puts it, because it determines whether Christianity shall be a religion of grace or of merit. For Luther, it touches 'the very heart of the gospel', says Anglican Evangelical theologian J. I. Packer. Indeed, 'The whole gospel of the grace of God . . . was bound up with it.' For Luther, Packer adds, it was 'the cornerstone of the gospel and the very foundation of faith'.[22] Packer summarizes the debate:

> Here was the crucial issue: whether God is the author, not merely of justification, but also of faith; whether, in the last analysis, Christianity is a religion of utter reliance on God for salvation and all things necessary to it, or of self-reliance and self-effort. Justification by faith only is a truth that needs interpretation. The principle of sola fide is not rightly understood till it is seen as anchored in the broader principle of sola gratia. What is the source and status of faith? Is it the God-given means whereby the God-given justification is received, or is it a condition of justification

[21] Luther, *The Bondage of the Will* (1525; London: James Clarke & Co. Ltd., 1957), p. 319.
[22] J. I. Packer, 'Historical and Theological Introduction', in Luther, *The Bondage of the Will*, pp. 41–3.

which is left to man to fulfil? Is it a part of God's gift of salvation, or is it man's own contribution to salvation? Is our salvation wholly of God, or does it ultimately depend on something that we do for ourselves?[23]

Erasmus' perspective was quite modern. He exalted human freedom. Belief that salvation depends upon the human will was consistent with his philosophy. Even so, he saw the issue as tiresome and divisive. Better to get on with the practical issues of life than to weary oneself in theological nit-picking, he thought. Luther correctly perceived that the issue was far more than theological nit-picking. The gospel, no less, was at stake.

Luther and the Reformers were careful to remove from salvation the last possible support of human merit. They affirmed that, while Christ is the ground or basis of our salvation, and faith is the instrumental means by which we receive salvation, the ultimate cause of our salvation is God's 'grace alone'. Faith does not save us. Christ does, on the basis of the unmerited mercy of God which he has shown toward us, the undeserving. Our response of faith is itself a part of God's gift of salvation. Far from being meritorious, faith is a gift. It is not our own. The Fall of man has left us in bondage to sin, with no capacity for faith. If we believe, it is because God has given us the ability to do so. The apostle Paul said,

> For by grace you have been saved through faith and that not of yourselves, it is the gift of God; not as a result of works, that no one should boast. (*Eph.* 2:8,9)

You are saved 'by grace . . . through faith'. What faith? The faith that is 'not of yourselves'. God gave it to us. Evangelicals affirm in addition to 'faith alone' God's unmerited mercy and 'grace alone'.

Grace alone reminds us that 'it is by his doing' that we are 'in Christ Jesus' (*1 Cor.* 1:30). If I believe, it is because God gives me the ability to believe. If I have chosen Christ, it is because he first

[23] Ibid., p. 59.

chose me (*John* 15:16). If I love Christ, it is because he first loved me (*1 John* 4:10). It was while I was dead and blind and ignorant and helpless that Christ died for me and then began to work decisively in my life (*Eph.* 2:1–7). The Reformers did not, and we must not, lose sight of the fact that it is by the sovereign, initiating, electing love of God in Christ that we are saved. Calvin, in his only statement regarding his conversion, which is found in the preface to his commentary on the Psalms, shows the biblical perspective on our salvation in saying,

> God, by the secret guidance of His providence, at length gave a different direction to my course . . . God by a sudden conversion subdued and brought my mind to a teachable frame, which was more hardened in such matters than might have been expected from one at my early period of life.[24]

Why am I saved? Because 'God so loved me'. And why did God so love? One can plunge no deeper than Deuteronomy 7:7 – He loves us because he loves us. Nothing we have done, nothing he might have seen or foreseen has attracted, earned, or merited his favour. Our salvation is of God's sheer mercy and grace alone.

God's Glory Alone (Soli Deo Gloria)

In 1528, Patrick Hamilton, a noble-blooded twenty-four year-old Scotsman returned home early from a period of study in Germany, a convert to Luther's gospel. He returned knowing that his new convictions meant certain death for him. For six weeks he preached, and as Knox said, 'Neither the love of life, nor yet the fear of that cruel death, could move him a jot to swerve from the truth once professed.'[25] He was arrested, tried and condemned. On 29 February 1528, Patrick Hamilton was burned to death in St Andrews. For six hours, on a cold and wet winter day the fire

[24] John Calvin, *Commentary on the Book of Psalms* (Edinburgh: Calvin Translation Society, 1845), p. xi.
[25] Beatrice M. Sawyer, *Seven Men of the Kirk* (Edinburgh: Church of Scotland Youth Committee, 1959), p. 11.

struggled to burn. Finally he cried out, 'Lord Jesus, receive my spirit.' Patrick Hamilton, who might have had all of life before him, came to a tragic end.

Eighteen years later, 28 February 1546, George Wishart – Reformed Protestant, mighty preacher of the gospel and the mentor of John Knox – was burned to death in front of St Andrews Castle. The little book, *Seven Men of the Kirk*, describes his moving end:

> When he came to the fire he prayed: 'Father of heaven I commend my spirit into Thy holy hands.' To the people he said: 'For the Word's sake, the true gospel given me by the grace of God, I suffer this day by men; not sorrowfully, but with a glad heart and mind. For this cause I was sent, that I should suffer this fire for Christ's sake. This grim fire I fear not. If persecution comes to you for the Word's sake fear not them that slay the body, and have no power to slay the soul.' The hangman knelt beside him and said: 'Sir, I pray you forgive me.' 'Come hither to me', he answered and kissed him on the cheek. 'Lo, here is a token that I forgive thee. My friend, do thy work.'[26]

What possesses men to do such things? Certainly this is where the previous point, and indeed all other points, have been leading us. The Reformers lived and died for Scripture alone, Christ alone, faith alone, and grace alone because they saw that these principles gave all of the glory to God and none to man. Indeed they understood that the goal of *everything* we do is to be God's glory – 'for from Him, and through Him, and to Him are *all things*, to Him be the glory forever and ever' (*Rom.* 11:36). 'All things': for the Reformers that meant that nothing was excluded from the pursuit of God's glory. Zeal for the glory of God led Luther and the Reformers into every sphere of life.

The reformation in the theology of the church quickly spilled over into the church's worship and form of government. Further it spilled over into family life, giving prominence to marriage and the Christian home. Still further it spilled over into society as educational, political, economic, and cultural institutions and

[26] Ibid., p. 25.

activities were reformed to the glory of God. No corner of existence was left untended by their pursuit of God's glory, in life and in death. But we shall have to wait for subsequent chapters to develop these thoughts more fully.

The Reformers were among the most humble, self-effacing, God-exalting men who ever lived. The Psalmist's cry, 'Not to us, O LORD, not to us, but to Thy name give glory' (*Psa.* 115:1) might be called the motto of the Reformation. Indeed *Soli Deo gloria* was the 'motto of mottoes' for them, as they sought not their own glory but God's.

Calvin, by his instruction, was buried in a simple pine box in an unmarked grave. His grave site is unknown to this day. Why? Lest anyone should be drawn to him and not to Calvin's God alone; lest in death anyone should make a hero of him and have his eyes drawn away from Calvin's Saviour, Jesus Christ.

We will review our Reformation heritage in the following pages because we wish to take our stand with the Reformers. The sequence of the 'solas' will be altered to follow the order of logic rather than the order of Luther's personal history, as in the preceding pages. Yet the principles, we trust, are the same: *sola Scriptura, solo Christo, sola fide, sola gratia,* and supremely, *soli Deo gloria.*

2

SOLA SCRIPTURA

2 TIMOTHY 3:16–17

Is there such a thing as a certain source of truth? Can we know right from wrong or distinguish truth from error? Alan Bloom opened his celebrated book, *The Closing of the American Mind*, with the statement: 'There is one thing a professor can be absolutely certain of: almost every student entering the university believes, or says he believes, that truth is relative.'[1]

He then went on to describe the contemporary intellectual climate as one in which there is no ability to distinguish good from bad, truth from error, even the important from the unimportant. All such distinctions are seen as being contrary to the chief virtue in today's world, that of openness. One must be open to all opinions, perspectives, and beliefs. Why? Because the truth cannot be known. Indeed there is no truth. Every viewpoint is as good and as valid as the next.

The West has been racing down this road of relativism for a long time. Steadily the moral foundation of Christendom has been eroded. Today our society is in a state of ethical chaos. Much of

[1] Alan Bloom, *The Closing of the American Mind* (New York, NY: Simon & Schuster, 1987), p. 25.

that chaos has been directly absorbed by the churches. Described by the Scripture as 'the pillar and support of the truth' (*1 Tim.* 3:15), the church more typically has become the mirror image of society, joining, rather than fighting, the chorus saying there is no truth, all is relative, and openness is the only virtue. Today we have church leaders endorsing fornication, homosexuality, and even under certain circumstances extra-marital affairs, because, after all, truth is relative and love is supreme. Who can know? We must, insist these church leaders, be open to alternative lifestyles. A few years ago Episcopal Bishop John Shelby Spong, in his book, *Living in Sin: A Bishop Rethinks Human Sexuality,* endorsed all of the above, announcing without shame, 'I stand ready to reject the Bible in favour of something that is more human, more humane, more life-giving, and, dare I say, more godlike.'[2] At the time many thought he was an extreme case. Today we know that his views have been adopted by the General Convention of the Episcopal Church USA, and the Methodists, Presbyterians, and Congregationalists are contemplating similar actions.

Where can we go to find valid answers to life's questions? Where can we go to find reliable, trustworthy, authoritative standards for faith and conduct? The radicals scoff at the asking of such questions. They see the quest for authoritative answers as a childlike refusal to deal with reality. Reality, they say, is a world in which we are on our own. We have to make our own way. They fear an outside authoritative source, preferring ethics by consensus. The answer of historic Christianity is *sola Scriptura,* to 'Scripture Alone'. God has spoken. He has not abandoned us. He has not left us to our own devices. We can do more than take polls and count votes. He has given the world the gift of Truth, found in his holy Word, the Bible. The Bible alone is *inspired* by God, it alone is *infallibly true,* and it alone is *authoritative.* There we find truths to believe and standards to follow.

[2] John Shelby Spong, *Living in Sin: A Bishop Rethinks Human Sexuality* (San Francisco: Harper & Row Publishers, 1988), p. 133.

The late medieval church raised the 'tradition' of the church to a place of authority equal to that of the Scripture. 'Tradition' included a host of extra-biblical practices and beliefs which had been received into the church over the centuries, whether by common acceptance or by the decisions of Popes and councils. 'Holy writ' and 'Holy tradition' were both accepted as authoritative sources of divine truth. Over both stood the church's magisterium, its infallible teaching office, to which belongs final authority in interpreting both tradition and Scripture. Opposing that position, the Reformers affirmed *sola Scriptura*. Scripture alone is to determine what we believe and what we do. They argued that to confer an authoritative status on the church or on tradition was contrary to the Bible's own self-testimony, contrary to the views of the early church, a novel idea that failed to gain acceptance until the twelfth century, and was not fully developed until as late as the fourteenth century.[3] Today many churchmen want to raise their finger to the wind and make popular opinion the rule for the church. Others bow before almighty science and give undisputed authority to its claims.

Let us, then, review together what we believe about the Bible, and why we stand in a long line of godly men and women who have said that 'Scripture Alone' is our rule of faith and practice.

Inspired by God

The Bible alone is 'inspired' by God. On this point both Rome and Protestants agreed. Whatever qualities one may wish to attribute to traditions, councils, other writings, or to prophecy today, they are not 'inspired' in the unique sense that Scripture is. We read in 2 Timothy 3:16: 'All Scripture is inspired by God and profitable for teaching, for reproof, for correction, for training in righteousness.' The words 'inspired by God' translate the Greek

---

[3] See Keith A. Mathison, 'Sola Scriptura' in R. C. Sproul, Jr., ed. *After the Darkness, Light* (Phillipsburg, NJ: Presbyterian & Reformed Publishing, 2003), pp 34,35. For more details see Keith A. Mathison, *The Shape of Sola Scriptura* (Moscow, Idaho: Canon Press, 2001), pp 1–121.

word, *theopneustos*, meaning literally, 'God-breathed'. The NIV translates it just so, reading, 'All Scripture is God-breathed.' It describes not the quality of the writings, but their *source*. It is not that the Bible is 'inspiring' (though it certainly is), but that it is a product of the creative breath of God. It describes, not our subjective response to a document – 'I find it inspiring' – but the objective truth about it – 'It comes to us from God.' Scripture is divine in origin. It comes to us from his mouth. The Bible is not just a collection of wise human sayings, it is God's wisdom for us.

Similarly Peter believed in the Bible's divine origin:

> But know this first of all, that no prophecy of Scripture is a matter of one's own interpretation, for no prophecy was ever made by an act of human will, but men moved by the Holy Spirit spoke from God (2 *Pet.* 1:20–21).

The Scriptures are not merely a human product, or 'an act of human will', he says. No, they were written by 'men moved by the Holy Spirit'. When they spoke, they 'spoke from God'. The word 'moved' (*pheromenoi*) is used in Acts 27:15 of a ship being driven along by the wind. B. B. Warfield, the great Princeton theologian and apologist of the late nineteenth and early twentieth centuries (1851–1921), said it indicates that the prophets were 'taken up by the Holy Spirit and brought by His power to the goal of His choosing'.[4]

The 'Higher Critical Theories' of the nineteenth-century have forced orthodox believers to spell out in greater detail what is meant by 'inspiration'. Some critics have sought to limit inspiration to a part of the Bible (for example, the Sermon on the Mount) and not the whole, because, the book of Jonah, for example, is such an embarrassment to 'thinking' people. Classic Protestants have insisted that inspiration is *plenary*, or of the whole. We are not in a position to pick out (and cast off) the

---

[4] B. B. Warfield, *The Inspiration and Authority of the Bible* (Philadelphia: Presbyterian & Reformed Publishing, 1948), p. 137.

uninspired parts from among the inspired, say the orthodox. All of the Bible is inspired. It is all God's Word. Other critics sought to accommodate so-called errors in the biblical record by arguing that the thoughts or ideas in the Bible were inspired, but not the words. Individual words could be uninspired and errant, but the thoughts behind the words were inspired. Against this untenable theory (how can we get to the thoughts except through the words?) the orthodox have insisted that inspiration is *verbal*, it extends to the words themselves, indeed to the 'jot and tittle', down to the individual letters (*Matt.* 5:18). Both plenary and verbal inspiration encompass the Bible's view of itself.

We do not believe that the Scriptures were dictated to the biblical writers, who acted as little more than secretaries, though sometimes that may have been the case (for example, *Jer.* 36:2–4; *Rev.* 1:11, 19). Rather, God worked in and through the unique circumstances and personalities of the biblical writers in such a way that their writings reflect their individual traits and gifts. The style of Paul's Greek is very different from that of John. My revered Old Testament teacher, J. A. Motyer, used to say that there was no Hebrew in all the world so beautiful as that of Isaiah. The biblical writers were hand-picked individuals with unique gifts. But when they wrote, each one wrote the very Word of God. The human and divine are united in Scripture. Jesus Christ, the Word made flesh, is truly God and truly man, yet without sin or error. Similarly the Bible unites the human and the divine, without error.

During the late nineteenth century, heated debates were taking place in the USA concerning the nature of biblical inspiration. C. A. Briggs (1841–1913) of Union Theological Seminary, New York, argued that the Word of God was like the pure light of the sun which, when passing through the human personality, was coloured, like sunlight through coloured glass. What we see through the glass may be beautiful, but it is not the pure Word, it is corrupted. Warfield took up this imagery and answered that when an artist creates a stained glass window, the effect when light passes through it is not a corruption, but a work of art. The artist so arranges things that the effect is exactly the one desired. So it is with divine inspiration. As it passes through the human personality it is coloured, but not corrupted. God created the human authors. He governed their development and so superintended their circumstances, that when they spoke or wrote, it was exactly what God wanted them to speak or write.[5]

That Scripture is the inspired Word of God is the Bible's self-attestation. Repeatedly we find that, as far as the biblical writers are concerned, what Scripture says, God says. 'Scripture says', 'It says', and 'God says', are used interchangeably.[6]

For example, Psalm 95:7 says,

> For He is our God, and we are the people of His pasture, and the sheep of His hand. Today, if you would hear His voice . . .

But the writer to the Hebrews, introducing his citation of this verse, says:

> Therefore, just as the Holy Spirit says, 'Today if you hear His voice . . .' (Heb. 3:7).

What Scripture says, God says. The words of the Psalm are not merely what David or the Psalmist says, but what 'the Holy Spirit says'.

Similarly, the Apostle Paul, citing words that Moses wrote in Genesis 12:1–3, where he records the words of God, attributes the words to 'Scripture'.

> And the Scripture, foreseeing that God would justify the Gentiles by faith, preached the gospel beforehand to Abraham, saying, 'All the nations shall be blessed in you' (*Gal.* 3:8; cf. *Acts* 4:25; *Matt.* 19:5).

What God said to Abraham can be described as Scripture personified. 'Scripture . . . preached'.

Another example may be found in Hebrews 10:5. Citing the words of Jeremiah 31:33, the writer to the Hebrews says, 'The

---

[5] Ibid., p. 156.
[6] Warfield wrote the definitive article on this, entitled 'It Says:' 'Scripture Says:' 'God Says:' found in *Inspiration and Authority*, pp. 299–350.

Holy Spirit also bears witness to us . . . saying,' (*Heb.* 10:15). What Jeremiah says the Holy Spirit says.

Finally, citing the words of Moses, Jesus says,

> Have you not read, that He who created them from the beginning made them male and female, and said 'For this cause a man shall leave his father and mother, and shall cleave to his wife; and the two shall become one flesh?' (*Matt.* 19:4–5).

Who 'said' these words of note? 'He who created them from the beginning.' What Moses wrote and Scripture says, God says.

The Scriptures are no less than 'the oracles of God' (*Rom.* 3:2), says the apostle Paul.

Our confidence is this: our Bible is the very Word of God. This is not the word of man. This is not merely a human book. This is God's Word and message to humanity, given by the verbal, plenary inspiration of the Holy Spirit.

Infallible and Inerrant

If inspiration is understood and accepted, the next point is, in one sense, redundant. If the Scripture comes to us from the mouth of God, then Scripture must be true. If *all* the Scripture comes to us from the mouth of God, it is *all* true. Jesus said this succinctly: 'Thy word is truth' (*John* 17:17). The church may err. People may err. Councils and Confessions may err. But Scripture does not err. The doctrine of the Scripture's inerrancy or infallibility is a necessary consequence of the doctrine of its inspiration. If the Scriptures are from God, they must be true, and all true, right down to the individual letters of each particular word. If they have come to us from God, who is himself all Truth, they must be free from error. On whatever subject the Scriptures touch, they speak truly, whether in the area of religion, history, science, psychology, or morals.

What about those in the broader church today who wish to deny the inerrancy of the Scripture? What do we say when they speak of the limitations of the human authors, of an ancient cosmology, of mistakes in historic detail, and of enculturation?

What do we say when they claim that the Bible is 'full of contradictions'?

Our conviction, and that of the church through the centuries, is that all limitations are perceived limitations, all mistakes are perceived mistakes, and all contradictions are perceived contradictions. They are perceived, not real. For every perceived problem, there is an answer, a solution, or a harmonization. The scholars have already resolved many 'problems', some of which were thought to be unanswerable as recently as the early twentieth-century. For the few that remain, we await the fresh insight which God will yet give. But we never locate the problem in the Bible. All problems are ultimately our problems: problems caused by mistakes in transmission (copyists' errors), poor translations, the limited understanding and abilities of interpreters, but not problems in Scripture itself.

John Gerstner (1914–96) Professor of Church History at Pittsburgh Theological Seminary, provided a fine survey of church history that leaves little doubt that the traditional Christian view is that the Bible is 'all true'. This was certainly the case with the early church Fathers (clearly seen in Origen, Ambrose, Clement of Alexandria, and Tertullian, some of whom came close to holding a theory of dictation).[7]

Augustine of Hippo (AD 354–430), whom Gerstner terms 'the great leader of the universal church' and 'probably the most important Christian theologian since Paul', was also 'the great leader on the inerrancy of Holy Scripture'.[8] Augustine wrote, 'I . . . believe most firmly that not one of those authors [of the Bible] has erred in writing anything at all.'[9]

Richard Lovelace, who provides another brief but useful survey of the historical view of the church, cites Augustine (Letter 82.3) as saying:

---

[7] John H. Gerstner, 'The Church's Doctrine of Biblical Inspiration', in James M. Boice, ed., *The Foundation of Biblical Authority* (Grand Rapids, Michigan: Zondervan, 1978), pp. 26–32.
[8] Gerstner, pp. 29, 32.　　[9] Gerstner, p. 32.

I most firmly do believe that the authors were completely free from error. And if in these writings I am perplexed by anything which appears to me opposed to truth, I do not hesitate to suppose that either the manuscript is faulty, or the translator has not caught the meaning of what was said, or I myself have failed to understand it.[10]

Augustine's conviction was the conviction of the Church Fathers, of the Medieval Church, of the Roman Catholic Church, of the Eastern Orthodox Church, and of the Reformers. Luther, among his many affirmations of inerrancy, said,

St Augustine, in a letter to St Jerome, has put down a fine axiom – that only Holy Scripture is to be considered inerrant.[11]

Inerrancy is the view of Calvin, Knox, the Protestant Scholastics of the seventeenth and eighteenth centuries, the Westminster Divines, American Puritans and Jonathan Edwards, American Presbyterianism until the turn of the twentieth-century, Southern Presbyterianism until the 1940s, and of worldwide conservative evangelicalism today. Universal, catholic Christianity has always believed the Bible to be the 'infallible rule of faith and practice'.

If some modern churchmen find this hard to swallow, their reluctance has more to do with their acceptance of worldly assumptions than it has to do with anything inherently wrong with the Bible. The modern world, with its bias against the supernatural, its hatred of external authority, its humanistic assumptions, scoffs at the idea of an inerrant Bible. Some churchmen find the spirit of the age to be irresistible. Admittedly the word 'inerrant' has something of a scientific awkwardness about it. In what sense is the poetry of the Psalms inerrant? The old word was 'infallible' or 'without error'. But again the champions of orthodoxy have been pushed by those who wish to

[10] Richard Lovelace, 'Inerrancy: Some Historical Perspectives', in Roger R. Nicole & J. Ramsey Michaels, eds. *Inerrancy and Common Sense* (Grand Rapids: Baker Book House, 1980), p. 20.
[11] John Warwick Montgomery, 'Lessons from Luther on the Inerrancy of Holy Writ', in Montgomery, ed. *God's Inerrant Word* (Minneapolis: Bethany Fellowship, Inc., 1973), p. 68.

accommodate errors into clarifying their meaning. A few years back some basically conservative theologians began to speak of the Bible as infallible in its teaching while errant in historical detail, cosmology, its view of origins, and so on. So the orthodox answered: the Bible is inerrant in all that it teaches, in whatever realm it addresses. Yet the games go on. Now some are speaking of 'limited inerrancy'. We, however, unashamedly stand in the mainstream of historic Christianity in affirming that the Bible is free from error in all that it affirms, it is the inerrant, infallible Word of God.

Authoritative

We have now reached the final two points to which we have been building. Because the Bible is the inspired Word of God and free from error, it is authoritative in all that it says. This really is the crux of the matter. At no point may a disciple of Christ decide to oppose the Bible and run his or her life based on his or her own set of standards rather than the those of the Bible. At no point may I legitimately deny its authority. I have a rule for faith and practice. I have a standard by which to judge my life. I have absolutes by which to live. Jesus said:

> For truly I say to you, until heaven and earth pass away, not the smallest letter or stroke shall pass away from the Law, until all is accomplished. Whoever then annuls one of the least of these commandments, and so teaches others, shall be called the least in the kingdom of heaven; but whoever keeps and teaches them, he shall be called great in the kingdom of heaven (*Matt.* 5:18–19).

Several of the categories with which we have concerns are addressed here. Jesus' words have enormous implications for our understanding the inspiration and truthfulness of the Bible. Jesus identifies even the smallest letter of Scripture as accurate and certain. But our main concern here is with authority. The written Word ('Law' has that breadth of meaning here) remains normative, Jesus declares, 'until heaven and earth pass away', or until the end of the world. R. T. France sees this phrase as an idiom for the inconceivable, perhaps something like our 'until hell freezes over'.[12] Until such time, 'Not the smallest letter or stroke shall pass away from the Law, until all is accomplished.' Until 'all' *what* 'is accomplished'? Until all the will of God revealed in the Scripture is accomplished: until all that Scripture predicts or foreshadows, until all it commands and requires. The 'smallest letter' is probably a reference to the Hebrew letter *yod*. The 'stroke' is probably the Hebrew letter *waw* or the *serif*, the name for the small extensions on Hebrew characters that distinguish similar letters from one another. Together, the references to heaven and earth and the smallest letter or stroke form 'a very emphatic assertion of the permanent validity of Scripture', says New Testament scholar Leon Morris.[13] All must be accomplished, meaning, 'The entire divine purpose prophesied in Scripture must take place; not one jot or tittle will fail of its fulfilment', says D. A. Carson.[14] Every word will be proven true. How long will they remain authoritative? Until 'heaven and earth pass away', until all that Scripture predicts and requires is fulfilled. How much of it remains authoritative? All down to the smallest mark on the smallest letter. In other words, Jesus affirms the authority of the whole Bible for all time.

Because the Scriptures are perpetually authoritative, they must be 'kept' and 'taught'. Even the smallest letter of Scripture is to be kept and taught. The root meaning of the word 'annul' is the word meaning, 'to loose' (*luo*). In this context it means to relax, or repeal, or set aside. Anyone who 'repeals' even the least of the Old Testament commandments and teaches others to do the same shall be ranked and regarded as 'least' in the kingdom of heaven.

---

[12] R. T. France, *Matthew* (Grand Rapids: Wm. B. Eerdmans Publishing Company, 1985).

[13] Leon Morris, *The Gospel According to Matthew* (Grand Rapids: Wm. B. Eerdmans Publishing Company, 1992), p. 110.

[14] D. A. Carson, 'Matthew', in Frank E. Gaebelein, ed. *The Expositor's Bible Commentary*, Volume 8 (Grand Rapids: The Zondervan Corporation, 1984), p. 146.

This admonition applies to the great commandments as well as the 'least' of them. The person who annuls the commandments is contrasted with whoever 'keeps' (*poieo*, to do or keep) and 'teaches' them. Annulling them is the opposite of doing and teaching them. Jesus wants them kept and taught. Underscoring his seriousness, Jesus warns that rank in the kingdom of heaven will be determined by our faithfulness to these commands. Whoever 'keeps and teaches' them 'shall be called great in the kingdom of heaven'. Jesus teaches that if we are to please our heavenly Father, we are to teach and keep the Bible's commandments, from the greatest of them to the least of them, every 'jot and tittle', until heaven and earth pass away. The Scriptures are the absolute authority for the people of God until the end of time.

One final reference: Jesus said, 'Scripture cannot be broken' (*John* 10:35). This statement follows the quotation, 'You are gods', from Psalm 82:6. Warfield pointed out that even the most 'casual clauses', like this one from out of the middle of the Psalms, are considered authoritative by Jesus.[15] It raises this point: If the Scripture is regarded as such by Jesus, how can we consider it any less authoritative and true? Can the disciples of Christ have a lower view of scriptural authority than he did?

The Role of Tradition

Several of my closest friends from seminary have joined the Roman Catholic church.[16] Their decision to do so required them to accept the 'Holy Tradition', that is, the oral tradition, both preserved by the church and evolving through the ages, as equally authoritative with Scripture. Our questions to them have been, 'Where do you see tradition function with that kind of authority within the Scripture itself? Does Jesus ever appeal to tradition? Do the apostles? Do they not rather in their many, many

[15] Warfield, *Inspiration and Authority*, p. 140.
[16] They include Scott Hahn, Jerry Matatics, Steve Wood, and Marc Grodi. Hahn has written of his conversion in *Rome Sweet Home: Our Journey to Catholicism* (San Francisco: Ignatius Press, 1993).

disputations appeal to Scripture alone?' 'You err,' Jesus tells them, 'in not knowing Scripture or the power of God' (*Matt.* 22:29). Though the New Testament is full of debates between Jesus and the Pharisees, Jesus and the Sadducees, Paul and the Judaizers, John and the incipient Gnostics, and so on, never do Jesus or the apostles appeal to tradition.

We actually see the opposite. Jesus and the apostles present a devastating critique of using tradition in place of Scripture. With his own mouth Jesus condemned the 'tradition of the elders' (*Matt.* 15:2), saying,

> Neglecting the commandment of God, you hold to the tradition of men . . .

> You nicely set aside the commandment of God in order to keep your tradition (*Mark* 7:8–9).

The 'commandment' of God must always sit in judgment on our traditions. Scripture must reign supreme over all ecclesiastical traditions.

However, it may be that Evangelical Protestants have not always expressed their view of the positive authority of *tradition*, *the church*, and *reason* as carefully or with as much subtlety as they ought. Each has a role to play in discerning the will of God. That role is subordinate to Scripture, but it is a positive role. Let's explore how each ought to function relative to scriptural authority.

Tradition can have a positive and important role in the lives of both individual believers and the church as a whole. Tradition, in its place, is useful. G. K. Chesterton (1874–1936), in his book *Orthodoxy*, refers to tradition as 'democracy extended through time', and as 'the democracy of the dead'.[17] Chesterton meant

---

[17] G. K. Chesterton, *Orthodoxy: The Romance of Faith* (New York: Doubleday, 1908, 1990), pp. 47–8. Chesterton continues, 'Tradition refuses to submit to the small arrogant oligarchy of those who merely happen to be walking about. All democrats object to men being disqualified by accident of birth; tradition objects to their being disqualified by the accident of death' (p. 48).

that we are part of a community that we have inherited from the past. On any given issue, the voice of the departed is heard through our tradition. Our ancestors passed on to us their ways of doing and seeing things. We call their ways *tradition*. It represents the wisdom of their age. This rich heritage of the past is one reason why we ought to be slow and careful about changing our traditions. Conversely, because tradition has stood the test of time, we ought to be sceptical about the wisdom of the present age whenever it departs from the ways of the past. Tradition represents the votes of the dead in our various endeavours.

Chesterton also said, 'Don't move a fence before you know why it was put there in the first place.' What was the fence restraining? What was it defining? What was it keeping out? What was it keeping in? Someone had a reason for the fence. Discover the reason for the fence and whether or not it is still needed before you tear it down, move it, or replace it.

Even in non-Christian societies tradition has done much to restrain evil and ameliorate the human condition. Alan Paton makes this point in *Cry, the Beloved Country*, through the voice of Jarvis' dead son. Jarvis, the rich white land owner, discovered in his son's papers this statement:

> The old tribal system was, for all its violence and savagery, for all its superstition and witchcraft, a moral system. Our natives today produce criminals and prostitutes and drunkards, not because it is their nature to do so, but because their simple system of order and tradition and convention has been destroyed. It was destroyed by the impact of our own civilization. Our civilization has therefore an inescapable duty to set up another system of order and tradition and convention.[18]

Modernity brought much good to Africa, banishing witchcraft, superstition and ignorance. But it also broke down tribal authority and custom and brought nothing to replace it. It cast out one demon and seven more took its place, leaving in its wake shattered families,

[18] Alan Paton, *Cry, the Beloved Country* (New York: Charles Scribner's Sons, 1948), p. 146.

crime, and violence. Modernity has had the same impact on Western society, breaking down its 'system of order and tradition and convention'. Tradition can be a common-grace blessing of God, restraining evil, strengthening families, educating children.

Tradition in the church can help preserve orthodoxy and orthopraxy, and prevent corruption. Sure, some have elevated tradition to a status equal to that of Scripture. Even among those who do not do so officially (as in 'Holy Tradition'), they may do so informally, refusing, ever, to change anything. Progressives have sometimes rightly mocked the so-called 'Seven Last Words of the Church': 'We've Never Done It That Way Before.' That kind of *traditionalism* is wrong. But there is a proper role for tradition that corresponds to that just described. We may refer to it as that of 'witness'. For example, we value knowing how the early church, the church of the 'Church Fathers', did things. We might encounter descriptions of church life and government in secular histories of that day or in Christian writings. We might study the liturgies of the second to fourth centuries. We value theses documents not as authorities in themselves, but as witnesses to the meaning of Scripture. The closer the tradition is to the time of Christ and the apostles, the greater value we place on it as a witness to what the apostles meant by what they wrote.

Similarly, we value the creeds of the early church and the writings of the church's greatest theologians across the centuries, not for their inherent authority but as wise and insightful witnesses to the meaning of the Scripture. We value their interpretation of Scripture as much as we do our own. Likewise, we value the convictions and practices of the Reformed tradition, a tradition of *sola Scriptura*, because we value the interpretations and applications of the Reformers, the Puritans, and the American Presbyterians.

So we honour tradition. We consult the past. We are not like the cults which claim that they have been the first to discover the truth. We are slow to depart from our ancestors' thoughts and ways. We rely heavily upon their insights.

This, it seems to me, is the proper role of tradition. It is a guide, a check, a safeguard, protecting the best of the past from the whims of the present. It is never an end in itself or an authority in itself. Tradition is always subordinate to Scripture. But it has an important role to play.

The Proverbs warn us not to move the 'ancient boundary that your fathers have set' (*Prov.* 22:28). Jeremiah warns against those who 'stumble from ancient paths, to walk in bypaths' (*Jer.* 18:15). God exhorts his people:

> Stand by the ways and see and ask for the ancient paths, where the good way is, and walk in it; and you shall find rest for your souls (*Jer.* 6:16).

Both the church and society have suffered enormously from abandoning this principle.

What ought we to do, then, when we encounter a traditional practice? The simple answer is, Honour it. Give honour to whom honour is due (*Rom.* 13:7). Then ask, 'Why is it there? Why did they do this and prohibit that?' Assume our forefathers had reasons and seek to understand why they thought their reasons were good. Finally, depart from tradition only when the case to do so is compelling.

The problem is not tradition itself, but the ease with which it becomes 'traditionalism'. Even the well-intentioned can subtly shift from scriptural authority to maintaining the tradition – guarding their way of doing things, or the way things have always been done, even to the extent that the tradition is given preference over Scripture itself. The Protestant Reformers believed this had happened in the medieval church. Tradition had become the lens through which Scripture was viewed. In practice it came to occupy a position *superior* to that of Scripture. We must be careful not to let our traditions 'close the Bible' even if we spell tradition with a small 't'. We must be on our guard not to mutter those infamous 'Seven Last Words of the Church', and, thereby, for the sake of perpetuating our traditions, close our eyes to the biblical correctives.

The Church

Similarly, while the church itself cannot be the final authority, it does have authority. Jesus has given the church the 'keys of the kingdom' and the power of 'binding and loosing' (*Matt.* 16:18; 18:18). The church is the institution authorized to preach the gospel and administer the sacraments (*Matt.* 28:18–20). This authorization implies the task of interpreting that gospel and its ordinances. This is authority aplenty!

As noted above, 'the church' is also the community of faith within which biblical interpretation takes place. The Reformers, classical Protestantism, and wise believers today have not encouraged biblical exposition in isolation. As Keith Mathison points out, the Reformers believed in *sola Scriptura*, not *solo*, that is, Scripture *alone*, not Scripture *only*, not Scripture in isolation from the church and its history. They repudiated the radicals and their hyper-individualism which placed 'the private judgment of the individual above the corporate judgment of the church'.[19] One ought constantly to be checking one's reading of Scripture against that of the whole church and interpreting one's reading within the boundaries of orthodoxy.

Yet the church is subject to the Word of its Lord. In the end we must say that tradition and church do not judge, but are judged, by Scripture. Scripture is the *norma absoluta*, the absolute norm.

Reason

Finally, while reason cannot be allowed to usurp the place of Scripture as the final and supreme authority in the church, it too has a subordinate role to play in knowing the will of God. Luther famously referred to reason as 'the devil's whore'. Unfettered reason, autonomous reason, reason which believes only the observable, the empirically verifiable, the 'reasonable' as defined by a closed system of cause and effect, is the death of revealed religion. Enlightenment-inspired whoredoms confirm Luther's

[19] Mathison in R. C. Sproul, Jr. (ed.) *After the Darkness, Light*, p. 37.

scepticism, as modernists have all but 'sold the ranch' (for example, the doctrines of the Trinity, the dual nature of Christ, substitutionary atonement, justification, inspiration of Scripture, traditional ethics, miracles, etc.) in the name of reason. Over the last hundred or so years 'the assured results of science' trumped orthodox Christian teaching at every turn. The conflict between faith and reason has been a rout, though it has been a pyrrhic victory. The 'mainline' denominations are now on the 'sideline', their churches empty while conservative churches are full. Why? Because they are unable to resist the latest 'politically correct' thing. The *zeitgeist* (spirit of the age) has robbed the church of its doctrinal content, its message, its spiritual power and its audience.

Yet, we value reason. We are to love God with all of our minds (*Matt.* 22:37). He invites us, 'Come, let us reason together' (*Isa.* 1:18). God's wisdom is 'reasonable' (*James* 3:17). The Bible cannot be understood without the application of reason to its contents (see below on Scripture's *sufficiency*). But reason must be subordinate to Scripture. Where they conflict, we are to humbly submit our minds to Scripture's supreme authority.

Let's review what might be the situation for many of us. In our weekly services we may recite the Apostles' Creed. This is a tradition. It is also a historic Creed. We recite it because we believe it faithfully represents the teaching of Scripture. But it is not our final authority in any matter of faith – Scripture is. We may belong to a Presbyterian church. There, the Session has governing authority. But the Session is not the final authority; Scripture is. Presbyterians will regularly cite the Westminster Confession of Faith and the Larger and Shorter Catechisms. They are traditions. They are historic. They are reasonable. But they are not the final authority. As wonderful as they are, they are not final. In fact they are called 'subordinate' standards, that is, subordinate to Scripture. So also are our denominations' books of church order and church constitutions. Yes, they are important. They have stood the test of time and are valuable. We learn from them and use them as guides. They are full of wisdom. But their authority is not final and they are subject to change.

Most churches have many fine traditions. Most church practices are reasonable. But tradition and reason are not the final authority in matters of faith and practice. If they were, Baptist, Congregational, and Presbyterian churches would not have organs or any musical instruments in their churches. Presbyterians didn't for over two hundred years. Some might applaud this. But neither would those churches have microphones, speakers, electric lights, or central heating and air-conditioning. 'The way things have always been done' has never been the principle upon which classic Protestants have decided these things. How then do we determine doctrine and policy and practice in the church? How do we settle disputes and controversies?

> The supreme judge by which all controversies of religion are to be determined . . . can be no other but the Holy Spirit speaking in the Scripture.[20]

We value tradition, the church, and reason. But our final authority is Scripture. We believe that the Bible is inspired by an all knowing and eternal God. It is true, and it is authoritative in all that it affirms. This leads us to our last point.

Sufficient

The apostles believed that, 'All Scripture is inspired by God and profitable for teaching, for reproof, for correction, for training in righteousness; that the man of God may be adequate, equipped for every good work' (2 *Tim.* 3:16–17).

All that we need in the way of doctrinal, moral, and ecclesiastical training is found in the Scripture. The sixty-six books of the Old and New Testaments are sufficient to equip the people of God 'for every good work'. Not just 'some good works'. Not just 'most good works'. No, the Bible equips us for every situation. The Bible is complete, unique, sufficient.

[20] *Westminster Confession of Faith*, I.x.

The case can be made that every corruption of biblical Christianity begins by compromising the principle of sufficiency. Every deviation from the Christianity established by Christ and the apostles begins by adding to the Bible or by taking away from it. Every deviation is the Bible plus or minus *something*.

For the Christian Scientists, it is the Bible plus Mary Baker Eddy's *Key*. For the Mormons it is the *Book of Mormon*. For the Jehovah's Witnesses it is the *Watchtower*. For the Seventh Day Adventists it is the revelations of Ellen White. For the Roman Catholics, it is tradition and the magisterium (the authoritative teaching function of the church, expressed through its hierarchy of Bishops and Popes). For modernists, it is reason, or common sense, or the latest scientific discoveries. Calvin's question of all practices and beliefs was this: 'By what word of God, by what revelation, by what example, is this done?'[21] Unless a practice comes from the Holy Scripture, it has no place in the church. Scripture alone determines our faith and practice. To depart from this position is to be guilty of the above-mentioned sins of the Pharisees who, 'neglecting the commandments of God . . . hold to the traditions of men' (*Mark* 7:8).

Back in 1977, just as the Council on Biblical Inerrancy was beginning its work, J. I. Packer was already announcing to his classes with amazing prescience his conviction that the real battleground over the following decades would not be over Scripture's inerrancy, but over its sufficiency. Hermeneutical magicians were already juggling texts in such a way as to demonstrate that the modern situation so differed from the ancient that the old Scriptural norms need not apply. The Bible is not an adequate guide in answering today's questions, they implied. It was this tendency that prompted Noel Weeks to write *The Sufficiency of Scripture*,[22] addressing not liberals who deny biblical infallibility, but conservatives who affirm it but deny its sufficiency.

---

[21] *Institutes*, III.v.10
[22] Noel Weeks, *The Sufficiency of Scripture* (Edinburgh: Banner of Truth, 1988).

Women's roles, sexual ethics, and ordination are suddenly up for grabs, as also are pragmatic ministry concerns, where the advice of Wall Street, Madison Avenue, and Hollywood (that is, business, marketing and entertainment industries), as well as the insights of our 'therapeutic' culture, are valued over those of the Bible by churches seeking to grow. 'The contemporary church's abandonment of *sola Scriptura*', says John MacArthur, Californian pastor and founder of The Master's Seminary, 'has opened the church to some of the grossest imaginable abuses – including honky-tonk church services, the carnival sideshow atmosphere, and wrestling exhibitions.'[23] 'Therapeutic technique, marketing strategies, and the beat of the entertainment world often have far more to say about what the church wants, how it functions, and what it offers, than does the Word of God', warned the signers of the Cambridge Declaration.[24]

We can build a convincing case for biblical inerrancy and authority. But if in the end we deny its sufficiency, treating Scripture like a scythe in an age of power mowers, an ox cart among eighteen-wheelers, storing it in an old barn where it collects dust, unused and unread, its authority is useless. If when we face the supreme challenges of our day we view the Bible, though 'religiously' inspirational, as a document written long ago and far away, and therefore unable to answer the complex questions we face today, then the Bible becomes a useless book unable to guide us where it really counts. Over against this growing scepticism we need to remind ourselves that the Scriptures are sufficient to meet the challenges of modern life.

Still we need to be as careful about what we are saying about the Bible's sufficiency as we are about the Bible's authority. Sometimes we may have affirmed sufficiency simplistically, or in

[23] John F. MacArthur, Jr., 'How Shall We Then Worship?' in John H. Armstrong (ed.), *The Coming Evangelical Crisis* (Chicago: Moody Press, 1996), p. 181.
[24] James M. Boice and Benjamin E. Sasse, eds. *Here We Stand: A Call From Confessing Evangelicals* (Grand Rapids: Baker Book House, 1996), p. 15.

a manner not adequately nuanced. Recently both David F. Coffin and T. David Gordon have written brief but suggestive articles on the 'insufficiency' of Scripture in order to underscore what is really meant by 'sufficiency'.[25] Mathison makes the obvious point about Scripture: 'It cannot read itself. It cannot preach itself. It cannot interpret itself.'[26] Their concern is that Scripture is sufficient to do what it is designed to do but not sufficient to do what it is not. Among their arguments are the following:

1. The Scriptures are sufficient to reveal the way of salvation only in conjunction with *the work of the Holy Spirit*, both in regeneration and illumination. This would be the reason behind the New Testament prayers for God to grant knowledge, discernment, wisdom and understanding (for example, *Eph.* 1:15; *Col.* 1:9; *Phil.* 1:9). It is also the reason why the Reformers reinstituted the prayer for illumination in the worship service prior to the reading and preaching of Scripture, and why we continue to use it today. 'We acknowledge the inward illumination of the Spirit of God to be necessary,' said the Westminster Divines, 'for the saving understanding of such things as are revealed in the Word.'[27]

2. The Scriptures are sufficient to reveal the whole truth of God only in conjunction with *God's revelation in nature*. Does nature reveal the truth of God? Certainly it does. All the works of God reveal something of the nature of God. The heavens, because God made them, declare the glory of God (*Psa.* 19:1). God's 'invisible

---

[25] David F. Coffin, Jr. 'The Sufficiency of Scripture and Modern Theophany: An Appreciative Critique and Alternate Course', in Joseph A. Pipa, Sr. and J. Andrew Wortman, eds. *Written for Our Instruction: The Sufficiency of Scripture for All of Life* (Taylors: Southern Presbyterian Press, 2001), pp. 153–83; T. David Gordon, 'The Insufficiency of Scripture' in *Reformation Today*, January/February 2002, Vol. 11, No. 1, pp. 18–23. Coffin cites Turretin's *Elenctic Theology* as a source of his qualifications.

[26] Mathison in Sproul, Jr. *After the Darkness*, p. 43.

[27] *Westminster Confession of Faith*, I.vi.

attributes, his eternal power, and divine nature are clearly seen, being understood through what has been made,' so that those who remain unbelieving are 'without excuse' (*Rom.* 1:20). Pagans are condemned for exchanging the 'natural function for that which is unnatural', the implication being that humanity is obligated to deduce the lessons of the natural order and discern the will of God from them (*Rom.* 1:26–27). Believers likewise are asked, 'Does not even nature itself teach you?' (*1 Cor.* 11:14).

The will of God may be discerned from the works of God, what he wants from what he made, his aim from his design. Indeed even some of the details of worship and church government 'are to be ordered by the light of nature, and Christian prudence', says the Westminster Confession of Faith.[28] Understood properly, the axiom 'all truth is God's truth' provides a proper perspective. The biologist, the chemist, the astronomer, the geologist, the mathematician are all uncovering new truths about creation and the Creator that are not found in Scripture, and yet are occasions for wonder and awe respecting the One who made the heavens and the earth.

3. The Scriptures are sufficient to reveal the truth and will of God only in conjunction with *the right use of reason*. As noted above, reason must be used to rightly interpret the Bible. We discern the meaning of the Bible not through mystical experience but through extensive thought and contemplation. This is true both for what Scripture says and what it implies.

Does an insistence upon rigorous study undermine the *perspicuity* of Scripture, a doctrine closely associated with sufficiency? Not at all. The Scriptures are *clear*. The perspicuity of Scripture is a cardinal doctrine of the Reformation for which we are grateful, and the denial of which led to the suppression of lay Bible reading by Rome for over four hundred years. Can the laity be trusted to read the Bible for themselves? Yes, because the Bible is fundamentally clear.

[28] *Westminster Confession of Faith*, I. vi.

John Knox, in his first of several meetings with Mary Queen of Scots, had this question put to him by her: 'You interpret the Scripture in one way, they in another. Whom shall I believe? Who shall be the judge?'.

Knox answered for all Bible lovers, and for us today:

> You shall believe God who speaks plainly in his Word. Further than the Word teaches you shall not believe the one or the other. The Word of God is plain in itself. If there is any obscurity anywhere, the Holy Spirit, who is never contrary to himself, explains it more clearly in other places. No one can remain in doubt, save those who remain obstinately ignorant.[29]

The Scriptures are clear enough that the ordinary Christian, without the aid of an ecclesiastical (or scholarly) magisterium, can understand their main thrust. This is not to say that there are not difficult texts in Scripture or difficult doctrines. But the greater part and the main message is simple and clear, and the difficult texts are explained more clearly elsewhere in Scripture. John says:

> And as for you, the anointing which you received from Him abides in you, and you have no need for anyone to teach you; but as His anointing teaches you about all things, and is true and not a lie, and just as it has taught you, you abide in Him. (1 John 2:27).

The ordinary believer, through the indwelling Holy Spirit and the right use of reason, can understand and apply the teaching of the Bible. Yet this does not mean that he need not work at it.

For example, there are those things not explicitly taught in Scripture that must 'by good and necessary consequence' be 'deduced' from Scripture.[30] Jesus condemned the scribes for not having deduced the doctrine of the resurrection of the dead from the verse, 'I am the God of Abraham, Isaac, and Jacob.' Note the

---

[29] William Croft Dickinson, ed., *John Knox's History of the Reformation*, Volume Two (New York: Philosophical Library, Inc.), p. 18. I have taken the liberty of modernizing the English.

[30] *Westminster Confession of Faith*, I. vi.

steps that reason must take to reach the doctrine of resurrection: 'am' is present tense, Abraham therefore must be alive; if alive, the dead must be raised (*Matt.* 22:23-33).

Believers must not fall into an unwarranted biblicism which, in the name of biblical authority, narrows the scope of its application to only that which the Bible explicitly states and not to that which it implies as well. This is a danger when the nature of Scripture is not understood. There is not a verse for every occasion. The Bible is not a book of detailed casuistry providing answers for every imaginable ethical question. No doubt some have wished that the Bible were such a book (for example, the Pharisees and their Talmudic descendants; the medieval theologians). Yet it still applies to every occasion. How so? It reveals general principles which, to be grasped, must be illuminated by the Holy Spirit, and, to be applied concretely in life, must be joined with reason and wisdom. The need of wisdom can be illustrated by this fact – almost all of life is lived between the lines of explicit biblical commands.

We can summarize our point in this way: The Scriptures are sufficient to reveal to us the truth and will of God when read in conjunction with biblical wisdom. Biblical wisdom can be defined as understanding the nature of things. To do so I must know the 'sacred writings', 'which are able to give you the wisdom that leads to salvation through faith which is in Christ Jesus' (*2 Tim.* 3:15).

But I must also discern the nature of the people and the situations I face. I am commanded to love my wife and children (*Eph.* 5:22–28; 6:1–4). In order to do so I must be a student of both Scripture (*1 Cor.* 13 would be a great start) and my family. The wise husband and father will discern the particular needs of each individual member of his family. He will love in a manner that is both biblical and suited to the distinctive personality of each.

The wise Christian will want to ask two questions of every situation, 'What does the Bible say about these things' and 'What is required of me given the nature of things' (the nature of God and the world that he has made).

Consider the exhortation to speak the truth in love (*Eph.* 4:15). How are we to fulfil this requirement? We must know the truth. That is one side of the equation. But the other side is to speak it 'in love'. What that means in any given circumstance requires correctly perceiving the nature of things. Who am I in relation to the one to whom I am speaking? If I am speaking to an older man, I am to speak to him as a father; if to a younger man, as a brother; if to an older woman, as a mother; if to a younger woman, as a sister (*1 Tim.* 5:1, 2). In other words, I must correctly perceive who I am, who they are, who I am in relation to them, what the occasion is, and what is needed. My words are to be edifying, meeting the 'need of the moment', which means that they are to be suited to the situation, giving 'grace to those who hear' (*Eph.* 4:29). To speak appropriately in any given situation requires wisdom. This is why it is possible to know lots of Bible and be a fool. One may know what the Bible says and yet not correctly perceive the nature of the things (the circumstances, the people involved), and so misapply its teaching at every turn.

Why does the wise farmer plant in the spring and harvest in the fall (*Prov.* 10:5, 20:4)? Not because there is a verse in the Bible that tells him to do so. He does so because he correctly perceives the nature of things and acts in harmony with it. Those who do not are fools. God wrote both books, the book of Special Revelation (the Bible) and the book of General Revelation (nature). As we have seen, the ungodly abandon the 'natural' for the 'unnatural' (Rom. 1:26, 27). They reject the lessons that nature teaches (1 Cor.11:14). We are wise only when we conform our lives to the reality that both books (nature and the Bible) reveal.

Let us explore this further. The Sixth Commandment forbids unrighteous anger, but not righteous anger. Yet at what point does righteous anger become unrighteous? No rule book can define that for us. No verse will spell that out. If the Seventh Commandment forbids lust and the Tenth coveting, at what point does admiration or appreciation cross the line into illicit desire?

At what point does modesty cross the line into immodesty? At what point does wise stewardship cross the line into extravagance and excess on the one hand, or miserliness on the other? At what point does charity cross the line into enabling? A thousand times a day we make decisions about how we will relate to people, our resources, our jobs, our God. We are commanded to love and be kind to our neighbours, to make wise use of our things, to work hard on our jobs, to rejoice and reverence our God. There is no book that can tell us at exactly what point we have either begun or ceased to do any of these things. We can only know them by the Holy Spirit and wisdom. The Scripture provides the essential reference points in its 'thou shall nots' and 'thou shalls'. But ninety-nine out of a hundred applications are beyond the verses themselves, in the land between the lines, where the Holy Spirit must lead and wisdom must instruct. Again, this is why we must pray for 'discernment', 'knowledge', 'wisdom', and 'understanding' (*Eph.* 1:15–19; *Phil.* 1:9–11; *Col.* 1:9–12).

God wants us to have wisdom so we can evaluate our choices in life and choose the ones that lead us down a path that glorifies him. The apostle Paul prays for the Philippians to have wisdom so that 'they may approve the things that are excellent' (*Phil.* 1:9). He prays for the Colossians to have it so that they may 'walk in a manner worthy of the Lord, to please Him in all respects, bearing fruit in every good work', and so on (*Col.* 1:10–12).

The irony today could not be more pronounced. Many professing Christians are making foolish lifestyle choices, and doing so in the name of the Bible! There is no verse to forbid it, and so, off they go, plunging ahead with foolish decisions with respect to marriage, parenting, recreation, entertainment, fashion, schooling, and so on. There is much foolishness abroad today. The antidote is *biblical* wisdom applied to *all* of life.

Where does this leave us? We are battered by the world and its myriad voices and diversity of choices. What is true? What is right? What is important? God has given us an *infallible* standard. It is absolutely trustworthy and reliable. It gives us the truth of

God regarding God himself, man, sin, salvation, eternity, ethics, values, and the proper perspective and outlook on life. It is of unsurpassed *authority* because it alone is the voice of God on earth, given to us by divine *inspiration*. It is sufficient, making us 'wise unto salvation', equipping us for 'every good work' (2 *Tim.* 3:15–17). It does so, not through hundreds of thousands of rules, but by giving us general truths which the Holy Spirit applies in such a way as to guide us wisely in every situation, circumstance, and decision of life.

3

SOLO CHRISTO

Scripture alone can authoritatively teach us the way of salvation, as we have seen. Where then does Scripture lead us? To the church? To the clergy? To the sacraments? 'At the centre of the whole Scripture (the) Reformers saw a person, namely, one person,' writes John Armstrong, 'the God-man, Christ Jesus.'[1] He calls *solo Christo* (on account of Christ alone) the 'central emphasis' of the entire Reformation movement.

> The person of Christ was the necessity behind the doctrinal formulations of *sola gratia* and *sola fide*.[2]

Faith alone, is faith *in Christ alone*. Grace alone, is the grace of God alone extended to us *in Christ alone*. Christ is the hub around which the doctrines of the gospel revolve. Once grasped, *solo Christo* drove the whole programme of reform in the church, as priests were redefined as pastors, plain robes replaced vestments, tables replaced altars, and the ministry of the Word replaced sacramentalism. By *solo Christo* the Reformers meant, and we mean, three things: he is *the only Saviour*, his is *the only Sacrifice*, he is *the only Mediator*.

---

[1] John H. Armstrong, '*Solus Christus*: The Wonder of Christ's Glory', in Armstrong (ed.) *The Glory of Christ* (Wheaton, Illinois: Crossway Books, 2002), p. 18.   [2] Armstrong, p. 18.

The Only Saviour

Jesus said, 'I am the way, the truth, and the life, no one comes to the Father but through me' (*John* 14:6). Notice the repeating of definite articles: *the* way, *the* truth, *the* life. He is the one and only way, the one and only truth, the one and only life. He states it positively, 'I am.' And he reinforces the positive with the negative, 'No one comes to the Father but through Me.' Jesus and Jesus alone, is the Saviour of the world. This is the apostolic perspective, declared by Peter as well: 'And there is salvation in no one else; for there is no other name under heaven that has been given among men, by which we must be saved' (*Acts* 4:12).

The Reformers and Catholics theoretically were of one mind on this point. Not so the contemporary world, to whom mainly we must address this principle. Our contemporaries are happy to say of our religious convictions, whatever they might be, How wonderful for you. Philosophically, they are relativists. What they mean is, 'What is true is what is true for you.' Of your moral convictions they are happy to say, 'What is right is what is right for you.' All religions and moral systems are of equal worth. None is superior to the rest. For contemporary people there is no final truth. There may be truth when it comes to the law of gravity, or the laws of thermodynamics, but not in religion and morals. The only requirement in religion is that one be sincere in one's beliefs. We are all on the same road to the same place, they say. Our differences are superficial.

This is orthodoxy for twenty-first-century secular man. Dare to say that there might be a single truth in religion and morals, and one is accused of arrogance ('You think you alone are right'), of bigotry ('and you think everyone else is wrong'), and intolerance. Belief in ultimate truth is heresy in the light of the present day orthodoxies of relativism, pluralism, and secularism.

Of course, contemporary people really do not believe this. After all, as Bloom points out, whatever they might say about the British colonization of India, nearly everyone is pleased that one very sincerely held Hindu practice, that of widow immolation (the gathering together of a man's possessions at his death, including his widow, and burning them), was forcibly stopped.[3] The ancient Canaanites sincerely believed that the way to appease their gods was to offer up their infant sons to them in fiery sacrifice. The ancient Aztecs offered up teenage girls as sacrifices. As many as ten thousand had their hearts carved out in a single day in order to satisfy the demands of their gods. The most avid relativists are perhaps ready to make some concessions to the absolutists. Some religions are more true than others.

Classic Protestantism asserts that God has revealed himself through the prophets and apostles and recorded that revelation in his Word. That Word reveals a plan of salvation which has at its heart the incarnation of the Son of God. This 'Son of God' is not merely a great man, even a divine man, but 'God the Son', the God-Man, the second person of the Trinity united to human flesh. He is the 'Saviour of the World'. What he does is not just of tribal or local significance, but of universal significance.

Can we prove that Jesus is divine? Probably not to the satisfaction of those determined not to believe. What we can do is proclaim Christ and urge others to 'taste and see', to investigate the life, teaching, and death of Jesus Christ, and see if they find in him the final and complete revelation of God (*Heb.* 1:1–3). See if they find in him One who addresses the human condition, the meaning of life, and human needs in a way that is compelling, even irresistible. Why do we believe? Because we have investigated and found the meaning of life in knowing Christ. He is the Compelling One.

JESUS' TEACHING

Consider His teaching. Those who heard Jesus were amazed, 'Never did a man speak as He did' (*John* 7:46). His Sermon on the Mount is considered the greatest sermon ever preached. Matthew records that when he concluded 'the multitudes were amazed at His teaching' (*Matt.* 7:28). They had heard the

---

[3] Bloom, *Closing of the American Mind*, p. 2.

Beatitudes, the most wonderful description of *godly character* ever given:

> Blessed are the poor in spirit, for theirs is the kingdom of heaven. Blessed are those who mourn, for they shall be comforted. Blessed are the gentle, for they shall inherit the earth. Blessed are those who hunger and thirst for righteousness, for they shall be satisfied. Blessed are the merciful, for they shall receive mercy. Blessed are the pure in heart, for they shall see God. Blessed are the peacemakers, for they shall be called sons of God (*Matt.* 5:3–9).

Poverty of spirit, meekness, humility, and mercy were not virtues in the ancient world. It was Jesus who made them desirable. He taught us to esteem these qualities.

Jesus gave them a glimpse of *mission*:

> You are the salt of the earth . . . You are the light of the world. A city set on a hill cannot be hidden . . . Let your light shine before men in such a way that they may see your good works, and glorify your Father who is in heaven (*Matt.* 5:13a, 14, 16).

This vision of the godly having a sanctifying influence upon individuals, families, and civilizations has inspired believers for generations. America's first 'founding father', John Winthrop (1588–1649), for example, drew upon this vision for the budding American civilization in 1630, in his sermon aboard the *Arbella* as it lay in Boston harbour. 'You shall be as a city upon a hill', he told his fellow colonists. 'The eyes of all people are upon you.'[4]

Jesus gave his disciples unparalleled *ethical instruction*:

> . . . but whoever slaps you on your right cheek, turn to him the other also. And if anyone wants to sue you, and take your shirt, let him have your coat also. And whoever shall force you to go one mile, go with him two . . . But I say to you, love your enemies, and pray for those who persecute you in order that you may be sons of your Father who is in heaven; for He causes His sun to rise on the evil and the good, and sends rain on the righteous and the unrighteous (*Matt.* 5:39b–41,44,45).

[4] Francis J. Bremer, *John Winthrop: America's Forgotten Founding Father* (Oxford: The University Press, 2003), p. 179.

The world had never heard of such a thing as love for one's enemy. Far more typical was the ethos, 'Love your neighbour and hate your enemy.' Jesus inspired a new ethic of love. His words were uniquely, we would say even supernaturally, insightful, inspiring, penetrating, and powerful. Never was this more the case than when he taught about religion.

He distilled the essence of *true religion*. Let me summarize.

First, Jesus taught that our aim in religion ought to be *pleasing God* not man.

> When therefore you give alms, do not sound a trumpet before you, as the hypocrites do in the synagogues and in the streets, that they may be honoured by men. Truly I say to you, they have their reward in full . . . And when you pray, you are not to be as the hypocrites; for they love to stand and pray in the synagogues and on the street corners, in order to be seen by men. Truly I say to you, they have their reward in full. But you, when you pray, go into your inner room, and when you have shut your door, pray to your Father who is in secret, and your Father who sees in secret will repay you (*Matt. 6:2, 5, 6*).

Jesus' words spelled the death knoll for external, formalistic religion forever. True piety, he insisted, aims to please God *from the heart* and *in secret*.

In conjunction with pleasing God, Jesus taught the greatest prayer ever prayed, the Lord's Prayer:

> Pray, then, in this way: 'Our Father who art in heaven, Hallowed be Thy name. Thy kingdom come. Thy will be done, On earth as it is in heaven. Give us this day our daily bread. And forgive us our debts, as we also have forgiven our debtors. And do not lead us into temptation, but deliver us from evil. For Thine is the kingdom, and the power, and the glory, forever. Amen' (*Matt. 6:9–13*).

It was Jesus who taught us to see God not as abstract power, not as an impersonal force, but as *Father*.

Second, Jesus taught that our aim in true religion ought to be *trusting God* and not things.

Do not lay up for yourselves treasures upon earth, where moth and rust destroy, and where thieves break in and steal. But lay up for yourselves treasures in heaven, where neither moth nor rust destroys, and where thieves do not break in or steal; for where your treasure is, there will your heart be also (*Matt.* 6:19–21).

No one can serve two masters; for either he will hate the one and love the other, or he will hold to one and despise the other. You cannot serve God and mammon (*Matt.* 6:24).

For this reason I say to you, do not be anxious for your life, as to what you shall eat, or what you shall drink; nor for your body, as to what you shall put on. Is not life more than food, and the body than clothing? Look at the birds of the air, that they do not sow, neither do they reap, nor gather into barns, and yet your heavenly Father feeds them. Are you not worth much more than they? And which of you by being anxious can add a single cubit to his life's span? And why are you anxious about clothing? Observe how the lilies of the field grow; they do not toil nor do they spin, yet I say to you that even Solomon in all his glory did not clothe himself like one of these. But if God so arrays the grass of the field, which is alive today and tomorrow is thrown into the furnace, will He not much more do so for you, O men of little faith? (*Matt.* 6:25–30).

But seek first His kingdom and His righteousness; and all these things shall be added to you (*Matt.* 6:33).

Were more beautiful words ever spoken? Was a more incisive, comprehensive summation of life ever given? Are his words not always contemporary, particularly suited to the materialistic, consumption-driven twenty-first-century?

This is just the tip of the iceberg. It was Jesus who warned his disciples about judgementalism:

Do not judge lest you be judged (*Matt.* 7:1).

It was Jesus who taught the 'Golden Rule':

Therefore, however you want people to treat you, so treat them, for this is the Law and the Prophets (*Matt.* 7:12).

We should not fail to mention his unforgettable parables: the Sower (*Matt.* 13), the Good Samaritan (*Luke* 10:30–37), the Prodigal Son (*Luke* 15:11–32), the Rich Man and Lazarus (*Luke* 16:19–31), the Rich Fool (*Luke* 12:16–21), and the Lost Sheep (*Matt.* 18:12–14; *Luke* 15:7), to name but a few.

Who could speak such words as these? This was no mere man. These words have the ring of divine truth about them.

JESUS' CLAIMS

Even more startling than Jesus' teaching were his claims. Listen to what he expected of those who heard his Sermon on the Mount:

> Therefore everyone who hears these words of Mine, and acts upon them, may be compared to a wise man, who built his house upon the rock. And the rain descended, and the floods came, and the winds blew, and burst against that house; and yet it did not fall, for it had been founded upon the rock. And everyone who hears these words of Mine, and does not act upon them, will be like a foolish man, who built his house upon the sand. And the rain descended, and the floods came, and the winds blew, and burst against that house; and it fell, and great was its fall (*Matt.* 7:24-27).

Who would say such things? Who would expect of others that they would 'act upon' his words, even building upon them, even claiming that failure to build upon the foundation of his words would be like choosing to build one's life/house upon sand?

The human heart finds life wearying. We are in a struggle to survive; work is burdensome. We are in a struggle against evil and the darkness of our own hearts. Sin creates wearisome trouble, confusion and complexity. Jesus says:

> Come to Me, all who are weary and heavy-laden, and I will give you rest. Take My yoke upon you, and learn from Me, for I am gentle and humble in heart; and you shall find rest for your souls. For My yoke is easy, and My load is light (*Matt.* 11:28–30).

Is this not an extraordinary claim? Jesus promises 'rest' for the 'weary and heavy-laden'. Yet is there not some inclination to believe that he can do it? It is remarkable that so few dismiss him outright as a fraud or a lunatic. We are compelled to take Jesus seriously.

Indeed, Jesus claimed to have the capacity to fulfil the deepest longings, aspirations and needs of the human soul. Is the human heart not empty, crying out for fulfilment? We try the world's commodities and they fail us. We indulge sensual pleasure; we accumulate material things; we achieve great success; we try chemical stimulants; and in the end, 'Nothing tastes', as Marie-Antoinette said of her sense-satiated existence. The soul remains unfulfilled, empty, unsatisfied. The soul was made for the eternal and it cannot be content with the merely temporal. Jack Higgins, an accomplished author, was once asked in an interview, 'What is it you know now that you wish you'd known as a boy?' He replied, 'That when you get to the top, there is nothing there.'[5] To the empty, hungry soul Jesus says, 'I am the bread of life; he who comes to Me shall not hunger, and he who believes in Me shall never thirst' (*John* 6:35).

Even more emphatically he invites us,

> If any man is thirsty, let him come to Me and drink. He who believes in Me, as the Scripture said, 'From his innermost being shall flow rivers of living water' (*John* 7:37b-38).

We know what it is for the body to be hungry and thirsty. We know the yearning, the craving to quench, to satisfy its appetites. It is an apt metaphor for the spiritual condition of our souls. There is that which corresponds to this in our hearts. The soul longs to have its hunger filled, its thirst quenched. Jesus identifies himself as the One who is able to do this. He makes a remarkable claim. He is the One who is able to satisfy the deepest needs of the human soul. He is *the* Bread of Life. He is the Water that is able to quench the thirst of every human heart.

We also experience confusion in this world. Our confusion fills us with anxious doubts and fears. We are not sure whether to go

---

[5] Quoted in Alister E. McGrath, *Intellectuals Don't Need God, and Other Modern Myths* (Grand Rapids, Zondervan, 1993), p. 15.

to the right or the left. We are not sure about what is right or wrong, or true or false. There are so many competing voices, so many opinions, so little consensus. Jesus says:

> I am the light of the world; he who follows Me shall not walk in the darkness, but shall have the light of life (*John* 8:12).

Light represents truth. Over against the confusion of competing claims Jesus provides certainty. Over against the darkness of sin and ignorance Jesus is (and provides) the light of purity and truth. Those who know Christ are delivered from the darkness and walk in the light of righteousness and truth. We know the truth and it sets us free (*John* 8:32). Rest for the weary, bread for the hungry, water for the thirsty, light for the ignorant – Jesus promises all these in himself.

JESUS' LIFE

We may add to Jesus' teaching and claims *the testimony of his life*. We can only provide a cursory survey (which we invite the reader to investigate), but Jesus' whole life demonstrates his unique and supernatural qualities.

His remarkable interaction with ordinary people: Nicodemus (*John* 3), the Samaritan Woman at the well (*John* 4:7–26), the woman caught in adultery (*John* 8:1–11), the Rich Young Ruler (*Matt.* 19:16–22), and the multitude on whom he felt 'compassion' (*Matt.* 9:36).

His shrewd training of the Twelve;

His wise and sometimes piercing responses to his opponents in debate: regarding the Sabbath ('The Sabbath was made for man not man for the Sabbath', *Mark* 2:27), tradition (*Matt.* 15:1–20), divorce ('What God has joined together let no man break asunder', *Matt.* 19:6), taxes ('Render to Caesar the things that are Caesar's and to God the things that are God's', *Matt.* 22:23–32), the greatest commandment (*Matt.* 22:34–40), the identity of Christ (*Matt.* 22:41–45), and the errors of the scribes and Pharisees (*Matt.* 23:1–39);

His miraculous feats that no one bothered to deny had taken place: Turning water into wine (*John* 2:1ff), walking on water (*Matt.* 14:22–33), stilling the storm (*Mark* 4:35–41), healing the sick, the lame, and blind (*Matt.* 15:29–31, etc.), raising the dead (*John* 11), feeding the Five Thousand (*Matt.* 14:13–21), and his own resurrection.

All must recognize the impact of Jesus' remarkable ministry. The historian H. G. Wells, not a Christian himself, was willing to concede the point:

> More than 1900 years later a historian like myself, who doesn't even call himself a Christian, finds the picture centring irresistibly around the life and character of this most significant man . . . The historian's test of an individual's greatness is 'What did he leave to grow?' Did he start men to thinking along fresh lines with a vigour that persisted after him? By this test Jesus stands first.[6]

The scholarly Christian historian Jaroslav Pelikan (b. 1923), in his *Jesus through the Centuries,* affirmed the importance of Jesus as a historical figure:

> Regardless of what anyone may personally think or believe about him, Jesus of Nazareth has been the dominant figure in the history of western culture for almost twenty centuries.[7]

With great eloquence two anonymous statements have affirmed the extraordinary influence of Jesus upon the life of this planet. The first, entitled 'One Solitary Life', concludes saying:

> All the armies that ever marched, all the navies that ever sailed, all the parliaments that ever sat, and all the kings that ever reigned, put together, have not affected our life on earth as much as that one solitary life.

The second, entitled 'The Incomparable Christ', beautifully elaborates on the impact of Jesus' life:

[6] Cited in Philip Yancey, *The Jesus I Never Knew* (Grand Rapids, Michigan: Zondervan Publishing House, 1995), p. 17.
[7] Quoted in John Stott, *The Incomparable Christ* (Downers Grove, IL: InterVarsity Press, 2001) p. 15.

More than nineteen hundred years ago there was a Man born contrary to the laws of life. This Man lived in poverty and was reared in obscurity. He did not travel extensively. Only once did He cross the boundary of the country in which He lived; that was during His exile in childhood. He possessed neither wealth nor influence. His relatives were inconspicuous and had neither training nor formal education. In infancy He startled a king; in childhood He puzzled doctors; in manhood He ruled the course of nature, walked upon the billows as if pavements, and hushed the sea to sleep. He healed the multitudes without medicine and made no charge for His service. He never wrote a book, yet all the libraries of the country could not hold the books that have been written about Him. He never wrote a song, and yet He has furnished the theme for more songs than all the songwriters combined. He never founded a college, but all the schools put together cannot boast of having as many students. He never marshalled an army, nor drafted a soldier, nor fired a gun; and yet no leader ever had more volunteers who have, under His orders, made more rebels stack arms and surrender without a shot fired. He never practised medicine, and yet He has healed more broken hearts than all the doctors far and near. Every seventh day the wheels of commerce cease their turning and multitudes wend their way to worshipping assemblies to pay homage and respect to Him. The names of the past proud statesmen of Greece and Rome have come and gone. The names of the past scientists, philosophers, and theologians have come and gone, but the name of this Man abounds more and more. Though time has spread nineteen hundred years between the people of this generation and the scene of His crucifixion, yet He still lives. Herod could not destroy Him and the grave could not hold Him. He stands forth upon the highest pinnacle of heavenly glory, proclaimed of God, acknowledged by angels, adored by saints, and feared by devils, as the living, personal Christ, our Lord and Saviour.

To these we can add the eloquent testimony of missionary and Yale scholar Kenneth Scott Latourette (1884–1968) from the seventh volume of his massive *A History of the Expansion of Christianity*:

In this world of men, with its aspirations and its struggles . . . there appeared one, born of woman . . . To most of . . . his contemporaries he seemed a failure . . . Yet no life ever lived on this planet has been so influential in the affairs of men. From it has grown the most nearly universal fellowship, the Christian church, that man has known . . . From that brief life and its apparent frustration has flowed a more powerful force for the triumphal waging of man's long battle than any other ever known by the human race. Through it millions have had their inner conflicts resolved in progressive victory over their baser impulses. By it millions have been sustained in the greatest tragedies of life and have come through radiant. Through it hundreds of millions have been lifted from illiteracy and ignorance, and have been placed upon the road of growing intellectual freedom, and of control over their physical environment. It has done more to allay the physical ills of disease and famine than any other impulse known to man. It has emancipated millions from chattel slavery and millions of others from exploitation by their fellows. It has been the most fruitful source of movements to lessen the horrors of war, and to put the relations of men and nations on the basis of justice and peace.[8]

This exceptional life, these extraordinary claims, these remarkable words, this unparalleled influence – what is one to make of it all? As Bishop Stephen Neill asked,

What kind of stone could it be that, once thrown into the pool of human existence, could set in motion ripples that would go on spreading until the utmost rim of the world had been reached?[9]

C. S. Lewis (1898–1963) thought long and hard about these things and commented on them frequently.[10] Lewis said:

---

[8] Quoted in John Stott, *The Incomparable Christ,* p. 164.

[9] John Stott, *The Cross of Christ* (Downers Grove, IL: InterVarsity Press, 1986) p. 65.

[10] Thankfully the editors of *The Quotable Lewis* have gathered these penetrating comments in one place. See Wayne Martindale and Jerry Root, eds., *The Quotable Lewis* (Wheaton, Illinois: Tyndale House Publishers, Inc., 1989).

Christians believe that Jesus Christ is the Son of God because He said so. The other evidence about Him has convinced them that He was neither a lunatic nor a quack.[11]

In other words, one is compelled by the life, teaching, and claims of Jesus to move in one of these two directions: either he is the Son of God or he is mad.

Listen to Lewis again:

The historical difficulty of giving for the life, sayings and influence of Jesus any explanation that is not harder than the Christian explanation, is very great. The discrepancy between the depth and sanity and (let me add) shrewdness of His moral teaching and the rampant megalomania which must lie behind His theological teaching unless He is indeed God, has never been satisfactorily got over. Hence the non-Christian hypotheses succeed one another with the restless fertility of bewilderment.[12]

On the one hand there is the 'shrewdness of His moral teaching' and on the other hand the 'rampant megalomania' of which he must be guilty if his claims about himself are not true. Jesus forces us to decide between these alternatives. We must render a judgment. We must choose one or the other.

Lewis pushes us again by eliminating compromise as an option:

I am trying here to prevent anyone saying the really foolish thing that people often say about Him: 'I'm ready to accept Jesus as a great moral teacher, but I don't accept his claim to be God.' That is one thing we must not say. A man who was merely a man and said the sort of things Jesus said would not be a great moral teacher. He would either be a lunatic – on a level with the man who says he is a poached egg – or else he would be the Devil of Hell. You can shut Him up for a fool, you can spit at Him and kill Him as a demon; or you can fall at His feet and call Him Lord and God. But let us not

[11] C. S. Lewis, *Christian Reflections*, edited by Walter Hooper (Grand Rapids, Michigan: Eerdmans, 1967), 'The Language of Religion' (1967), p. 137.

[12] C. S. Lewis, *Miracles* (New York: Macmillan, 1960), Chapter 14, pp. 108–9.

come with any patronizing nonsense about His being a great human teacher. He has not left that open to us. He did not intend to.[13]

This brings us back to the question of why we believe our Bibles. When we examined *sola Scriptura* we were mainly concerned to demonstrate what Christians are to believe about the Bible and how it is to function in their lives. What about an unbeliever? He has doubts about the Bible's truthfulness. What do you say to him? We say, 'taste and see' (*Psa.* 34:8). Encounter the Jesus of the Bible and see if you do not hear the voice of the Shepherd (John 10:27). How do you know if Jesus really said what the Bible says he said? The simplest answer is, it would take a Jesus to invent a Jesus. If Jesus had never lived, one author insists, we would not have been able to invent him.[14] Behind Jesus' matchless words, deeds and extraordinary influence is someone whom the

---

[13] C. S. Lewis, *Mere Christianity* (New York: Macmillan, 1962), Book II, pp. 55–6. Lewis makes a similar statement in *God in the Dock: Essays on Theology and Ethics,* edited by Walter Hooper (Grand Rapids, Michigan: Eerdmans, 1970), p. 157–8: 'On the one side clear, definite moral teaching. On the other, claims which, if not true, are those of a megalomaniac, compared with whom Hitler was the most sane and humble of men. There is no half-way house and there is no parallel in other religions. If you had gone to Buddha and asked him, "Are you the son of Bramah?" he would have said, "My son, you are still in the vale of illusion." If you had gone to Socrates and asked, "Are you Zeus?" he would have laughed at you. If you had gone to Mohammed and asked, "Are you Allah?" he would first have rent his clothes and then cut your head off. If you had asked Confucius, "Are you Heaven?" I think he would have probably replied, "Remarks which are not in accordance with nature are in bad taste." The idea of a great moral teacher saying what Christ said is out of the question. In my opinion, the only person who can say that sort of thing is either God or a complete lunatic suffering from that form of delusion which undermines the whole mind of man. If you think you are a poached egg, when you are looking at a piece of toast to suit you, you may be sane, but if you think you are God, there is no chance for you. We may note in passing that He was never regarded as a mere moral teacher. He did not produce that effect on any of the people who actually met Him. He produced mainly three effects – Hatred – Terror – Adoration. There was no trace of people expressing mild approval.'
[14] Walter Wink, cited in Philip Yancey, *The Jesus I Never Knew,* p. 23.

world had not seen before and shall never see again. Either a gospel writer made him up, which would make that writer the most important person who ever lived, or he recorded what he actually saw and heard – One whom the writers of Scripture later called 'the Lord of Glory' (*1 Cor.* 2:8). This is what we have found. We invite you to him.

The Only Sacrifice for Sin

Jesus is the only Saviour, and his death on the cross is the only sacrifice that can pay the debt of our sin. How does Jesus save? By his death on the cross. How does the cross save? Why? How does it work?

Let us lay the foundation once more. A holy God does not wink at sin. He upholds a just, moral order. Sin demands punishment. 'The soul that sins, it shall die' (*Ezek.* 18:4); 'the wages of sin is death' (*Rom.* 6:23). Forgiveness requires death as well: 'Without the shedding of blood there is no remission of sin' (*Heb.* 9:22). Jesus Christ died my death on the cross. 'Luther was the first theologian to give prominence to the thought that the satisfaction to God for sin which . . . Christ rendered on our behalf on the cross, was *penal* and *substitutionary* in its nature' (my emphasis), says Packer.[15] Let us elaborate.

SUBSTITUTIONARY

First, His death was *substitutionary*. Jesus said he gave his life 'a ransom for many' (*Mark* 10:45). He died 'for' or 'on behalf of' (Greek *anti*) many. He died in their place. His blood of the new covenant was 'shed *for* many' (*Mark* 14:24), that is, on their behalf, in their place, for their benefit. Similarly, Paul said,

> For the love of Christ controls us, having concluded this, that one died for all, therefore all died (*2 Cor.* 5:14).

---

[15] J. I. Packer, *Honouring the People of God: Collected Shorter Writings of J. I. Packer, Volume 4* (Carlisle, Cumbria: Paternoster Press), p. 7.

He says 'one died *for* all', and, therefore, in him 'all died'. Jesus died as our representative (*Rom.* 5:12-21; *1 Cor.* 15:20-22). As our representative, he stood in our place. The punishment due to us was meted out to a substitute, a replacement.

PENAL

Second, Jesus' death was *penal*. By 'penal' we mean having to do with legal punishment for crimes committed, the penalty required for breaking the law of God. As our substitute, he bore our guilt and the judicial penalty our guilt incurred. The demands of the just law of God the Judge were fulfilled in Christ. Compare these verses:

> For what the Law could not do, weak as it was through the flesh God did: sending His own Son in the likeness of sinful flesh and as an offering for sin, He condemned sin in the flesh (*Rom.* 8:3).

> He made Him who knew no sin to be sin on our behalf, that we might become the righteousness of God in Him (*2 Cor.* 5:21).

> Christ redeemed us from the curse of the Law, having become a curse *for us* – for it is written, 'Cursed is everyone who hangs on a tree' (*Gal.* 3:13).

The apostle Paul (the writer of these verses) says that God 'condemned sin in the flesh', in Christ. This means that he rendered a judicial verdict condemning the sin of sinners. The sinless one came to 'be sin'. He did so 'on our behalf, that we might become the righteousness of God in Him'. Luther spoke of the 'wonderful exchange' that took place on the cross. He became 'a curse *for us*', bearing the curse of the Law, the judgment that the Law required. He did this 'for us', as our substitute.

> Surely *our griefs* He Himself bore, and *our sorrows* He carried; yet we ourselves esteemed Him stricken, smitten of God, and afflicted. But He was pierced through for *our transgressions*, He was crushed for our iniquities; the chastening for *our well-being* fell upon Him, and by His scourging we are healed (*Isa.* 53:4-5).

He who was delivered up because of *our transgressions*, and was raised because of our justification (*Rom.* 4:25).

But God demonstrates His own love toward us, in that while we were yet sinners, Christ died *for us* (*Rom.* 5:8).

He who did not spare His own Son, but delivered Him up *for us* all, how will He not also with Him freely give us all things? (*Rom.* 8:32).

For Christ also died for sins once *for all*, the just for the unjust, in order that He might bring us to God, having been put to death in the flesh, but made alive in the spirit (*1 Pet.* 3:18).

Christ died, these texts teach us, that he might bear *our* griefs, carry *our* sorrows. He was pierced for *our* transgressions and crushed for *our* iniquities. Christ died for *us*, he was delivered up *for us*. The sacrifice of Christ was a propitiating, justice-satisfying, wrath-quenching event. By his death the justice of God was satisfied. We are 'justified', says the apostle Paul,

as a gift by His grace through the redemption which is in Christ Jesus; whom God displayed publicly as a propitiation in His blood through faith. This was to demonstrate His righteousness, because in the forbearance of God He passed over the sins previously committed; for the demonstration, I say, of His righteousness at the present time, that He might be just and the justifier of the one who has faith in Jesus (*Rom.* 3:24–26).

The propitiation is 'in Christ Jesus' and 'in His blood' or by His death. Notice the phrase, 'just and justifier' in verse 26. The cross so satisfies the demands of justice that God is demonstrably 'just', that is right and uncompromising in his judicial activity, and 'justifier'. A 'justifier' is one who declares another to be just or righteous. Together they mean that God remains 'just' even as he justifies, pardons, and forgives those who have 'faith in Jesus'. The cross makes it possible for God to forgive and not compromise the requirements of justice in the process. The apostle John wrote the same:

> My little children, I am writing these things to you that you may not sin. And if anyone sins, we have an Advocate with the Father, Jesus Christ the righteous; and He Himself is the propitiation for our sins; and not for ours only, but also for those of the whole world (*1 John* 2:1–2).

> In this is love, not that we loved God, but that He loved us and sent His Son to be the propitiation for our sins. Beloved, if God so loved us, we also ought to love one another (*1 John* 4:10–11).

Christ offers in Himself ('He Himself', the apostle John says emphatically) the propitiation 'for our sins'. God 'sent His Son' for this very purpose.

Let us say it again: God forgives sinners without compromising justice (by overlooking sin) because Jesus Christ died in our place and thus satisfied divine justice. Thus, we speak of *penal or judicial substitution*. He paid the penalty which we owe. All believers say with the apostle Paul, Jesus Christ 'loved me, and delivered Himself up *for me*' (*Gal.* 2:20).

Let the impact of Christ's substitution sink in. On one otherwise ordinary day, John 'Rabbi' Duncan (1796–1870), nineteenth-century Professor of Hebrew at New College, Edinburgh, was lecturing his students on the subject of the atonement from Isaiah and Psalm 22. Suddenly overcome by the wonder of it all, he asked his students:

> Ay, ay, d'ye know what it was – dying on the cross, forsaken by His Father – d'ye know what it was? . . . It was damnation – and damnation taken *lovingly*.[16]

Lovingly Christ bore our sin and took our penalty. J. I. Packer, in his incisive booklet, *What Did the Cross Achieve? The Logic of Penal Substitution,* quotes Luther's dramatic and exuberant remarks:

> All the prophets did foresee in spirit, that Christ should become the greatest transgressor, murderer, adulterer, thief, rebel, blasphemer,

[16] A. Moody Stuart, *The Life of John Duncan* (1872; repr. Edinburgh: Banner of Truth, 1991), p. 105.

etc., that ever was . . . for he being made a sacrifice, for the sins of the whole world, is not now an innocent person and without sins . . . our most merciful Father . . . sent his only Son into the world and laid upon him the sins of all men: Be thou Peter that denier; Paul that persecutor, blasphemer and cruel oppressor; David that adulterer; that sinner which did eat the apple in Paradise; that thief which hanged upon the cross; and, briefly, be thou the person which hath committed the sins of all men; see therefore that thou pay and satisfy for them. Here now cometh the law and saith: I find him a sinner . . . therefore let him die upon the cross.[17]

When we contemplate the cross (which, I trust, we do with some frequency) we should ponder the love of God who rescues us, the unworthy. Christ suffered as he did *for me*. My sins put him there and gladly did he bear them. Our classic hymn writers repeatedly return to this theme with a sense of wonder at the love of God. Note the question that is raised:

> Was it for sins that I have done
> He groaned upon the tree?
> Amazing pity, grace unknown,
> And love beyond degree.

These are the words of Isaac Watts (1674–1748), the 'father of the English hymn'. If Christ 'groaned' for 'sins that I have done', then this is a remarkable thing! This is 'amazing pity, grace unknown, and love beyond degree'. Charles Wesley (1707–88), the 'sweet singer' of Methodism, asks the same question:

> And can it be that I should gain
> An int'rest in the Saviour's blood?
> Died He for me, who caused His pain?
> For me, who Him to death pursued?
> Amazing love! How can it be
> That Thou, my God, shouldst die for me?

---

[17] J. I. Packer, *What Did the Cross Achieve? The Logic of Penal Substitution* (Leicester: Theological Students' Fellowship, 1974), p. 32, n. 33. The quote is from Luther's *Galatians*.

Who crucified Christ? Our older hymn writers understood what we may have forgotten – our sins nailed Christ to the cross. I 'caused His pain' and 'to death pursued' him. If this is true, then I might ask with surprise 'And can it be that I should gain?' This is 'amazing love!' 'How can it be?, I ask. Perhaps most emphatically of all is the second stanza of 'Ah, Holy Jesus, How Hast Thou Offended':

> Who was the guilty
> Who brought this upon Thee?
> Alas, my treason,
> Jesus, hath undone Thee.
> 'Twas I, Lord Jesus,
> I it was denied Thee;
> I crucified Thee.

This is exactly the point. 'I crucified Thee.' Or we can look to the hymn, 'Hallelujah, What a Saviour!'

> Bearing shame and scoffing rude,
> In my place condemned He stood,
> Sealed my pardon with His blood:
> Hallelujah! What a Saviour!

If 'in my place condemned He stood,' if 'bearing shame and scoffing rude,' if he 'sealed my pardon with His blood', then what can we say? 'Hallelujah! What a Saviour!'

COMPLETE

Thirdly, his sacrifice, because it was the sacrifice of the Son of God and because it was substitutionary and penal, was *complete*. By complete we mean final and sufficient. By complete we mean never needing to be repeated or supplemented. The writer to the Hebrews said,

> For it was fitting that we should have such a high priest, holy, innocent, undefiled, separated from sinners and exalted above the heavens; who does not need daily, like those high priests, to offer up

sacrifices, first for His own sins, and then for the sins of the people, because this He did once for all when He offered up Himself (*Heb.* 7:26–27).

Because of who he is as our high priest, 'holy, innocent, undefiled,' and so on, and what he sacrificed, 'He offered up Himself', could not but be 'once for all'. Again, the writer says, '. . . but He, having offered one sacrifice for sins for all time, sat down at the right hand of God' (*Heb.* 10:12).

Unlike the Aaronic priests of the Old Covenant, who repeatedly offered sacrifices, it was only necessary that he should offer himself 'one sacrifice for sins for all time', and so he 'sat down'. His work was finished.

His atoning sacrifice was a once-for-all accomplishment. In his death he bore all the sins of all his people throughout the whole of world history. 'It is finished', Jesus said from the cross (*John* 19:30). His sacrifice needs no supplementation. Nothing may be added to it. The death of Jesus was complete, totally sufficient to atone for all of our sins.

As noted, this insight drove the whole work of Reform, transforming the church's understanding of the gospel and Christian ministries. To begin with, because Scripture teaches that the death of Jesus was complete (final and sufficient), the Reformers rejected the medieval concept of the mass as a sacrificial offering.

The position of Rome, articulated by the Council of Trent (1545–63), reaffirmed by Vatican II (1962–5), was that 'the sacrifice of the Mass is propitiatory, both for the living and the dead', and even that the Lord is 'appeased by the oblation thereof' (Session 22, chapter II).[18] The Council of Trent also anathematizes the following:

> Canon I: If any one saith, that in the mass a true and proper sacrifice is not offered to God; or, that to be offered is nothing else but that Christ is given us to eat: let him be anathema.

[18] Philip Schaff, *The Creeds of Chrystendom*, *Vol. II* (1889; repr. Grand Rapids: Baker Book House, 1985), p. 179.

Canon III: If any one saith that the sacrifice of the mass is only a sacrifice of praise and of thanksgiving; or, that it is a bare commemoration of the sacrifice consummated on the cross, but not a propitiatory sacrifice; or, that it profits him only who receives; and that it ought not to be offered for the living and the dead for sins, pains, satisfactions, and other necessities: let him be anathema.[19]

This doctrine of the Mass denied the finality and sufficiency of the sacrifice of Christ if the cross is in need of continual supplementation through the altar. Communion is a Supper, said the Reformers, not a sacrifice (*1 Cor.* 11:20). It is served upon 'the table of the Lord', not an altar (*1 Cor.* 10:21). His sacrifice was once for all and anything that weakens our sense of its finality robs it of its glory.

The Reformers rejected the terms 'priest' and 'altar' as appropriate for Christian ministry. Priests clothed in vestments offer sacrifices upon altars. Christian clergy are pastors or ministers dressed in simple robes who feed and tend God's sheep through the ministry of God's Word.

They rejected the 'treasury of the saints' as superfluous. Nowhere does Scripture mention such a treasury. Moreover, one need not go to saints for merits (even if they had any - they do not), because Christ's merits are sufficient.

They rejected the doctrine of Purgatory, where the souls of believers are alleged to go to be purged of the guilt and stain of unpaid (or unatoned) sins. In Christ there are no unpaid sins. For the believer, Christ's sacrifice covers *all* his sins for *all* time. Moreover death is final. 'It is appointed unto man once to die, and then the judgment' (*Heb.* 9:27).

They rejected the sale of 'indulgences', whereby one could purchase the benefits of the treasury of merit thereby reducing one's temporal punishments in Purgatory. Merits are not for sale. They are freely reckoned to our account in Christ.

They rejected prayers for the dead, because, as Calvin put it, 'The entire law and the gospel do not furnish so much as a single

[19] Ibid., pp. 184–5.

syllable to pray for the dead.'[20] They did not pray for the dead because the dead are in eternity. Their future is sealed. Either by Christ's sacrifice they are in heaven or because of rejecting him they have descended into hell. His sacrifice was once for all and sufficient for all our sins! The whole ministry of the church is transformed by one's view of the finality and sufficiency of Christ's atonement.

The Only Mediator

So far we have seen that Christ is the only *Saviour*, and his is the only *Sacrifice*. Our third principle of *solo Christo* is that Jesus is the *only Mediator*. A mediator is one who intercedes on behalf of alienated persons. How do I receive the benefits of what Jesus Christ did on the cross? Can I go directly to God for them? No. The gulf between God and man is too great. God is pure and holy and cannot tolerate a sinner like me. The benefits of death must be mediated to me through another. Who, then, can go to God for me? Who can plead my case before God? Who can ensure that the merits of Christ are credited to my account and my sin to his? Only one can mediate for me – Jesus Christ himself.

The apostle Paul writes,

> For there is one God, and one mediator also between God and men, the man Christ Jesus (*1 Tim.* 2:5).

Likewise the writer to the Hebrews says that Christ as our mediator intercedes for us.

> Hence, also, He is able to save forever those who draw near to God through Him, since He always lives to make intercession for them (*Heb.* 7:25).

We are able to 'draw near to God' directly because of Christ's mediation; 'He always lives to make intercession' for us. To whom do I turn to get what I need from God? Who can assist me in my search for the forgiveness of my sins and peace of conscience?

[20] *Institutes*, III.v.10

The answer given by Scripture, Reformers and believers today is 'Christ alone'. He alone mediates the blessings of redemption. He alone justifies. He alone forgives. He alone sanctifies. He alone adopts us into the family of God. I go directly to God through Jesus Christ. I need no celestial mediators, such as angels or saints or Mary; I need no earthly mediators such as clergymen and priests.

As our Mediator, he is our Advocate. John says,

> My little children, I am writing these things to you that you may not sin. And if anyone sins, we have an Advocate with the Father, Jesus Christ the righteous; and He Himself is the propitiation for our sins; and not for ours only, but also for those of the whole world (1 John 2:1–2).

John sees Jesus Christ as our Mediator, advocating on our behalf by pleading our case on the basis of his own work, his propitiatory sacrifice 'for our sins'. The apostle Paul envisions much the same:

> Who will bring a charge against God's elect? God is the one who justifies; who is the one who condemns? Christ Jesus is He who died, yes, rather who was raised, who is at the right hand of God, who also intercedes for us (Rom. 8:33–34).

If anyone (for example, the devil) should try to 'bring a charge' against us, to demonstrate from our record that we ought to be condemned, Jesus himself is interceding at the right hand of God on our behalf. 'He who died' is the same as he who 'intercedes' and defends.

As our Mediator Christ *ensures our salvation*. The Apostle Paul taught this in Romans 4:25. He said that Jesus was 'delivered up because of our transgressions'. By his death he paid the penalty of our sins. But he went on to say, 'and was raised because of our justification'. What does he mean? Paul means that Christ was raised so that he might ensure the application of the benefits of his death to our account. Christ's death *accomplished* our salvation, but his resurrection ensured that what he had accomplished would be *applied*. By his continual intercession

Christ ensures that all those for whom he died shall come to faith in him, be justified, adopted, sanctified, shall persevere, and, ultimately, be glorified.

In addition, as our Mediator Christ *guarantees our prayers*. We are taught to pray 'in Jesus name'. Why? Because he is the guarantor of access to the throne of grace. He is our high priest, so we may 'draw near with confidence to the throne of grace, that we may receive mercy and may find grace to help in time of need' (*Heb.* 4:16). We even 'have confidence to enter the holy place by the blood of Jesus' (*Heb.* 10:19; see also *Eph.* 3:13).

My close friends from seminary who converted to Roman Catholicism have justified their Mariolatry on the basis of folk-wisdom: if you want something from a great person, do not go directly, but instead enlist his mother in your cause. As at the Wedding Feast, ask Mary to ask Jesus (*John* 2:1–5). They would say your chances are better with Mary on your side. Jesus will not turn her down. Similar justification is offered for praying to the saints. Though my friends go to great lengths to deny it, I still ask, does this not inevitably undermine Jesus' mediatorial office? Does he not invite a direct approach? Does he not invite us to come to him (for example, *Matt.* 11:28–29)? Not so much as a syllable of Scripture commends the mediation of another. Jesus alone is the Mediator. For this role he is entirely sufficient and without need of assistance. Believers should not look to priests, nor to the sacraments, nor to the church, nor to the saints, nor to Mary, but to Jesus Christ alone.

The role of Christ as the sole Mediator has significant implications for the church and for individual believers.

First, the pastorhood of clergy and priesthood of all believers.
Because Christ is our priestly Mediator, we can see again why clergy in the Reformed and Protestant understanding are not priests but pastors or ministers. As such they do not attempt to do what Christ has already done. They do not offer sacrifices on altars. Neither do they stand between the people and God. They

do not have a special status or exercise special powers. Confessions of sin are not made through them, but directly to Christ. They are 'functionaries'. They are called by God and congregations to perform the functions of preaching, leading in worship, and administering the sacraments (*Acts* 6:1–7; *1 Tim.* 3; *Titus* 1:7–9). But they are not of a different order from other Christians. All believers are priests. The Reformers taught the 'priesthood of all believers'. We are 'a royal priesthood' (*1 Pet.* 2:9; see also *Rev.*1:6). 'All of us who have been baptized are priests without distinction,' said Luther, and 'those whom we call priests are ministers.'[21] Over three hundred years later New Testament scholar J. B. Lightfoot (1828–89) said the same thing in his celebrated essay on 'The Christian Ministry', placed as an appendix at the back of his commentary on Philippians. He said of the kingdom of Christ:

> It has no sacred days or seasons, no special sanctuaries, because every time and every place alike are holy. Above all it has no sacerdotal system. It interposes no sacrificial tribe or class between God and man, by whose intervention alone God is reconciled and man forgiven. Each individual member holds personal communion with the Divine Head. To Him immediately he is responsible, and from Him directly he obtains pardon and draws strength.

'All Christians are priests alike', he said.[22] As priests, all Christians are

> being built up as a spiritual house for a holy priesthood, to offer up spiritual sacrifices acceptable to God through Jesus Christ (*1 Pet.* 2:5).

All believers should offer sacrifices, but in this case we are the sacrifice. All Christians are exhorted to perform the priestly task of presenting themselves as 'living sacrifices' to God:

> I urge you therefore, brethren, by the mercies of God, to present your bodies a living and holy sacrifice, acceptable to God, which is your spiritual service of worship (*Rom.* 12:1).

[21] Bainton, p. 138. Quoted from Luther's *The Babylonian Captivity.*
[22] J. B. Lightfoot, *St. Paul's Epistle to the Philippians* (1868; repr. Lynn, Mass.: Hendrickson Publishers, 1981), p. 182, 185.

All Christians offer not a material, bloody sacrifice, but a 'sacrifice of praise':

> Through Him then, let us continually offer up a sacrifice of praise to God, that is, the fruit of lips that give thanks to His name. And do not neglect doing good and sharing; for with such sacrifices God is pleased (*Heb.* 13:15–16).

We all have the privilege of going directly to God through Christ without the assistance of human (or celestial) intermediaries. We all stand on level ground at the foot of the cross.

Second, the dignity of 'secular' vocations.

The socio-religious implications of the 'priesthood of all believers' are far-reaching. Because every believer is a priest, wrote John Leith (1919–2002), Professor of Theology at Union Theological Seminary in Virginia, every believer is accountable for himself before God. The distinction between clergy and laity disappears.

> No priest or institution can answer for any human being. Every human being is accountable. Every person must believe for himself because every person dies by himself.[23]

The individual, individual conscience, and individual responsibility are all given fresh emphasis. Not only does *solo Christo* imply the abolition of the distinction between priest and people, but also, Leith pointed out, 'the distinction between sacred and secular work'. He summarized,

> A person's daily work is not something done in addition to being a Christian or in spite of being a Christian. A Christian's daily work is one of the ways in which the Christian lives out his Christian faith.[24]

There is an essential equality among believers, both clergy and non-clergy. A proper understanding of vocation or calling

[23] John H. Leith, *Introduction to the Reformed Tradition* (Atlanta: John Knox Press, 1977), p. 113.
[24] Leith, p. 113.

developed from this. Against the medieval view of higher and lower callings, with priests and monks at the top and shopkeepers at the bottom, came an understanding of the dignity of the labour of one who fulfils his God-given vocation, whether it be as a preacher or a ditch-digger. Christian people toil in their 'secular' jobs working 'heartily', knowing 'it is the Lord Christ whom [they] serve' (*Col.* 3:23–24). The impact of this outlook on the prosperity of western, Protestant nations has been debated, but is no doubt immense.[25]

Christ is the only Saviour, his is the only sacrifice, and he is the only Mediator. Luther, Bucer, Knox, and all the Reformers understood these things, but none more so than Calvin, with whose moving words we close:

> We see that our whole salvation and all its parts are comprehended in Christ (*Acts* 4:12). We should therefore take care not to derive the least portion of it from anywhere else. If we seek salvation, we are taught by the very name of Jesus that it is 'of him' (*1 Cor.* 1:30). If we seek any other gifts of the Spirit, they will be found in his anointing. If we seek strength, it lies in his dominion; if purity, in his conception; if gentleness, it appears in his birth. For by his birth he was made like us in all respects (*Heb.* 2:17) that he might learn to feel our pain (cf. *Heb.* 5:2). If we seek redemption, it lies in his passion; if acquittal, in his condemnation; if remission of the curse, in his cross (*Gal.* 3:13); if satisfaction, in his sacrifice; if purification, in his blood; if reconciliation, in his descent into hell; if mortification of the flesh, in his tomb; if newness of life, in his resurrection; if immortality, in the same; if inheritance of the Heavenly Kingdom, in his entrance into heaven; if protection, if security, if abundant supply of all blessings, in his Kingdom; if untroubled expectation of judgment, in the power given to him to judge. In short, since rich store of every kind of good abounds in him, let us drink our fill from this fountain, and from no other.[26]

[25] Max Weber, *The Protestant Ethic and the Spirit of Capitalism* (New York: Charles Scribner's Sons, 1958); R. H. Tawney, *Religion & the Rise of Capitalism* (New York: Harcourt, Brace & Co., 1926); Michael Novak, *The Spirit of Democratic Capitalism* (New York: Simon & Schuster, 1982). See also Chapter 6 of the present work.   [26] *Institutes*, II.xvi.19.

4

SOLA FIDE

ROMANS 3:21–4:9

How may a man be made right before God? We are justified by faith alone (*sola fide*), in Christ alone (*solo Christo*), the Protestant Reformers answered. This conviction – *sola fide* – based upon *solo Christo*, was the principal cause of the sixteenth-century call to reform the church. Justification 'by faith alone, in Christ alone' has historically been recognized, according to J. I. Packer, 'as one of the two basic and controlling principles of Reformation theology'. He explains,

> The authority of Scripture was the *formal* principle of that theology, determining its method and providing its touchstone of truth; justification by faith was its *material* principle, determining its substance.[1]

Packer employs the categories of logic to help us distinguish the core of the Reformation debate. The 'formal' dimension of an argument has to do with its 'form', that is, with the rules of debate, the sources from which arguments can be drawn, the authorities that are to be regarded as legitimate. The Protestants argued that *Scripture alone* was the final authority in the debate. The Roman

[1] J. I. Packer, 'Introductory Essay', in James Buchanan, *The Doctrine of Justification* (London: Banner of Truth, 1961), p. 1.

Catholics argued that the church, its hierarchy, its tradition, and its normative interpretation of Scripture were sources that could also be cited as equally legitimate. Agreement was never reached on the 'formal' issue, and Protestants and Roman Catholics remain divided today over which sources are regarded as authoritative in theological debate.

The 'material' issue, the core theological 'matter' over which they disagreed, was that of justification. Again, Roman Catholics and Protestants could not agree about either the nature of Christ's atonement or the means by which its benefits are received. But it was the heart of their debate.

Calvin described the doctrine of justification by faith alone as 'the principal hinge on which religion turns',[2] and Luther described it as the *articulus stantis vel cadentis*, 'the article by which the church stands or falls'.[3] It was his conviction that,

> This article is the head and cornerstone of the Church, which alone begets, nourishes, builds, preserves and protects the Church; without it the Church of God cannot subsist one hour.[4]

It was this article of faith more than any other which brought the Reformers into conflict with medieval Roman Catholicism. 'It was the substantive and core issue of the debate', says R. C. Sproul.[5] Calvin, in his debate with Cardinal Sadoleto (1477–1547) said justification by faith was 'the first and keenest subject of controversy between us'. Remove the knowledge of this doctrine, he argued, and 'the glory of Christ is extinguished, religion is abolished, the church destroyed, and the hope of salvation utterly overthrown'.[6] It was faithfulness to this article of faith that

[2] *Institutes*, III.xi.1.

[3] This saying has long been attributed to Luther, though a later Lutheran theologian, Valentius Loescher, who used the expression in 1718, may be responsible for this exact formulation.

[4] Quoted by Sinclair B. Ferguson, *Know Your Christian Life* (Downers Grove, Illinois: Inter-Varsity Press, 1981), p. 71.

[5] R. C. Sproul, *Faith Alone: The Evangelical Doctrine of Justification* (Grand Rapids: Baker Book House, 1995), p. 18.

[6] Henry Beveridge, ed., *Selected Works of John Calvin: Tracts and Letters* (1844; repr. Grand Rapids: Baker Book House, 1983) p. 41.

determined the outcome of the conflict. 'At the beginning of our preaching,' Luther said,

> the doctrine of Faith had a most happy course, and down fell the Pope's pardons, purgatory, vows, masses, and such like abominations, which drew with them the ruin of all Popery . . . And if all had continued, as they began to teach and diligently urge the article of Justification – that is to say, that we are justified neither by the righteousness of the Law, nor by our own righteousness, but only by faith in Jesus Christ - doubtless this one article, by little and little, had overthrown the whole Papacy.[7]

Luther correctly saw that if sinners are justified by faith alone in Christ alone, then the whole system of salvation rooted in priest-operated, church-based religious works would collapse. A new, Christ-centred, faith-based Christianity would arise from its ashes.

Not only was *sola fide* central to the Reformation and its success, but it still addresses the fundamental question that each of us must answer today. After all, life is short and eternity is long. One day I will stand before God. I cannot escape this encounter. It *will* take place. How can I be made right in his eyes? Or to give the question a biblical ring, 'What must I do to be saved?' Answer: 'Believe in the Lord Jesus Christ and you shall be saved' (*Acts* 16:30–31). Believe. We are 'made right' not by living a moral life (it would never be moral enough), or by good works (they would never be good enough), or by religious deeds (they would never be pious enough), but by faith alone in Christ alone.

We should not view this conflict as a remote history lesson, unrelated to ministry. It is instead the heart of the gospel and the key to mission today. Since the Reformation every subsequent season of fruitful ministry has seen a renewed emphasis on justification by faith alone. The preaching of the great evangelists, whether John Bunyan (1628–88), George Whitefield (1714–70),

[7] Quoted in Buchanan, *Justification*, p. 23.

John Wesley (1703–91), Jonathan Edwards (1703–58), or Charles Spurgeon (1834–92) demonstrate this to be the case. No other doctrine so illustrates the sinfulness of man and the futility of his efforts to save himself. No other doctrine so glorifies Christ as the sole ground of our salvation. No other doctrine so establishes the security of the believer in Christ. Hence, no other doctrine is so vital to biblical preaching and effective ministry.

Regrettably, one may have to search long and hard to hear a sermon on the subject. The shelves of bookstores are not bursting with books dealing with justification by faith alone. Those that do deal with it are not on the best-sellers list. The writers of the Cambridge Declaration claimed that *sola fide* 'is often ignored, distorted, or sometimes even denied by leaders, scholars, and pastors who claim to be evangelical'.[8] Perhaps most of the blame for this can be placed on the nature of the age in which we live. The contemporary audience is reluctant to think theologically. It wants experience. It wants sensations. But it typically does not want to think, or think hard, or think in theological categories.

We are beginning to pay a price for our neglect. Twice in the last twenty-five years controversies have erupted in relation to the doctrine of justification. First, the 'Shepherd Controversy' convulsed Westminster Seminary in Philadelphia from 1975–82, resulting in the dismissal of Norman Shepherd from the faculty. O. Palmer Robertson recently has published his rebuttal of Shepherd, first written in the 1980s but not published until 2003, under the telling title of *The Current Justification Controversy*. He gave it this title because of the 'ongoing character of the original debate twenty years later', as he explains in the Foreword. Shepherd erroneously maintained that both faith and works are the instruments of justification. Robertson notes with alarm that such a debate should be occurring 'within the very womb of evangelical Christianity'.[9]

[8] Boice and Sasse (eds.), *Here We Stand*, p. 17.
[9] O. Palmer Robertson, *The Current Justification Controversy* (Unicoi, Tennessee: The Trinity Foundation, 2003), p. 10.

The second of these debates centres around the work of N. T. Wright and E. P. Sanders and the 'New Perspective' theologians. These professedly evangelical scholars declare that justification, as the apostle Paul defined it, has to do, not with individuals personally being declared righteous in Christ, but with membership in the covenant community. They deny, in other words, a forensic or judicial understanding of justification, its character as a declaration, the imputation of Christ's right-eousness, and the resulting personal salvation.[10] To be justified, they say, is to be rightly related to God through membership in the covenant community.

The influence of the 'New Perspective' men seems to be growing even in the most conservative evangelical circles. Moreover, there would appear to be some cross-fertilization between the followers of Shepherd and those of N. T. Wright, compounding this threat to the gospel.

It is crucial that we again give witness to *sola fide*, to justification by faith alone, that we might see the blessing of God upon our proclamation, as he has blessed it so often in the past.

A Necessary Doctrine

Justification by faith is a thoroughly biblical doctrine. One can fairly say that two New Testament books are devoted primarily to it. Chapters 1–8 of the Letter to the Romans were written as an exposition of 'justification by faith alone'; chapters 9–16 as a response. Galatians was written as a polemic in defence of the doctrine of justification.

In Romans chapters 1–3, Paul writes of the theological realities which undergird justification by faith, making it a *necessary* doctrine. We learn that it is necessary because of the nature of both God and man. God is our Judge. He is righteous. His 'wrath' is revealed against all human sin (1:18). His law-standard is

[10] For a brief and easy-to-read review of the issues see Charles E. Hill, 'N. T. Wright on Justification', *Third Millenium Magazine Online* (Vol. 3, Number 22, May 22 to June 3, 2001).

unachievable. Man is a rebel, a law-breaker, a moral and religious failure and hopelessly lost. This description applies to both Gentile (1:18–32) and Jew (2:1–3:8). Look at the Gentile record and what do you find: 'unrighteousness, wickedness, greed, malice' (1:29–32). And the Jewish record? It is no better.

> You, therefore, who teach another, do you not teach yourself? You who preach that one should not steal, do you steal? You who say that one should not commit adultery, do you commit adultery? You who abhor idols, do you rob temples? You who boast in the Law, through your breaking the Law, do you dishonour God? For the name of God is blasphemed among the Gentiles because of you, just as it is written (*Rom.* 2:21–24).

Drawing his indictment together, Paul summarized, 'both Jews and Greeks (Gentiles) are all under sin', indeed,

> There is none righteous, not even one; there is none who understands, there is none who seeks for God; all have turned aside, together they have become useless; there is none who does good, there is not even one (*Rom.* 3:10–12) .

With this sweeping indictment of the human race, the apostle has condemned us all. Gone are all our pretensions of moral and religious goodness. Gone are our claims of self-righteousness. Gone are our self-congratulating self-portraits as 'honest seekers' after truth. 'There is none righteous.' There is none who does good.' There is none who seeks for God.'

Where does this place us in relation to God? His 'wrath is revealed from heaven against all ungodliness and unrighteousness of men' (1:18). Our situation is not just bad, it is hopeless. We are condemned as transgressors and 'without excuse' (1:20). The standard of God's righteousness is beyond our grasp and his sanctions promise our destruction.

What can we do? Nothing but close our mouths. For two full chapters in Romans, 1:18–3:18, Paul's argument has had one aim – to shut our mouths – 'that every mouth may be closed, and all the world may become accountable to God' (3:19).

Without excuse and without virtue, we stand silent, condemned.[11]

How may we be saved? How may we stand before God? The gospel teaches that whatever we do in order to get right with God will not work. Our obedience is not pure enough. Our love is not earnest enough. It does not matter how many times we go to church, or say the creed, or put money in the plate. All our attempts are futile. They are worthless. Our religion will not save us. Our morality will not save us. There is nothing we can do to escape destruction. Our efforts to make ourselves right with God are completely futile; he is too holy, and we are too corrupt.

If we are to get right with God we must seek righteousness, not in ourselves, but in the direction of the clue given to us back in Romans 1:17 – in the righteousness that is 'of God' or 'from God' (the grammarians call this a 'genitive of origin'). This righteousness comes to us from God and is received 'from faith to faith'. In other words, its reception begins and ends with faith, or, as Cranfield, in his superb commentary on Romans, interprets it, 'by faith alone'. Justification, he says, 'is a righteousness which is God's gift,' given 'altogether by faith'.[12] The holiness of God and the wickedness of man make this, of necessity, the only viable way for sinners to be saved.

Justification

What, then, can be done about our hopeless situation? We are under condemnation (*Rom.* 5:16,18; see also 8:1). We need the opposite of condemnation. We need pardon and forgiveness. More precisely, we need to be justified or acquitted. Is this possible? How can we be made right before God? The Apostle Paul tells us:

[11] Charles E. Hill says against the 'New Perspective' slant on Romans 1–3 that, 'The question at hand here is not the question of who is to be called the people of God or who belongs in the covenant. Sin, or the wrath of God against sin, is the immediate problem – and this problem is faced by Jews who are in the covenant as well as by Greeks who are not' (Ibid., p. 4).
[12] C. E. B. Cranfield, *A Critical and Exegetical Commentary on the Epistle to the Romans, Vol. 1* (Edinburgh: T&T Clark Limited, 1980), p. 100.

> But now apart from the Law the righteousness of God has been manifested, being witnessed by the Law and the Prophets, even the righteousness of God through faith in Jesus Christ for all those who believe; for there is no distinction; for all have sinned and fall short of the glory of God, being justified as a gift by His grace through the redemption which is in Christ Jesus (*Rom.* 3:21–24).

The Apostle Paul says that there is a 'righteousness of God' which one may have 'through faith in Jesus Christ'. Yes, 'all have sinned.' That is the problem from which we cannot extract ourselves. Yet, one may be 'justified as a gift by His grace through the redemption which is in Christ Jesus'. Let us discern several distinctions in what he says.

THE NATURE OF JUSTIFICATION

First, *justification is a forensic or judicial act of God*. That is, it is a legal or judicial declaration by God whereby, as the *Shorter Catechism* says, 'He pardoneth all our sins and accepteth us as righteous in His sight.' 'Justification', says old Princeton Theologian A. A. Hodge (1823–86), 'is a judicial act of God.'[13] We will return to this theme repeatedly, merely stating for now that justification is a declaration, not a process; it reveals a new status, not a new nature; it is the verdict of the Judge, not the works of the accused; it is received through faith in Christ, not by the performance of meritorious works.

THE GROUND OF JUSTIFICATION

Second, *the ground of our justification is Jesus Christ*. We will return to the means by which we receive justification – faith – in a moment. For now, we focus on the ground or basis. The 'gift' of justification, says the apostle Paul, is given 'through' or on the basis of 'the redemption which is in Christ Jesus' (3:24). The basis of God's judicial act in pardoning sinners is the death of Christ.

[13] A. A. Hodge, *Outlines of Theology*, (1878; repr. Edinburgh: Banner of Truth, 1972), p. 498.

Imagine, for a moment, that you are a young boy at a county fair. Your father goes to the booth where he throws darts at balloons and, if he pops them all, he wins a prize. Your father steps up to the line, throws his darts and pops every balloon! He wins the prize, and he proudly brings it over to you and places it into your hands. Now answer the question, How did you come to have the prize? Do you have it because you opened your hand and received it? Yes, that is true. But your hand was only the instrument by which you received it. You and your hand deserve, receive, no credit for possession of the prize. The real reason, or ground, of your prize-receiving was your father's prize-winning. His accomplishments secured the gift and made its possession possible for you.

Similarly, the ground of our salvation is the work of Jesus Christ. It is not faith *per se* (the means) that saves, but faith in Jesus Christ (the ground) that saves. Our faith is not in faith. Regrettably many are confused about this. They attribute saving power to faith, believing, or so they seem to say, that as long as one has 'faith', regardless of the object of that faith, one is safe. 'Faith' in this scheme takes on a life of its own. It can be placed in (literally) anyone or no one! Warfield was right when he said: 'It is not, strictly speaking, even faith in Christ that saves, but Christ that saves through faith.'[14] His life and work secured our salvation. What did he do? We looked at this in detail in the previous chapter. We may again refresh our memory.

The New Testament uses a variety of terminologies to describe Christ's work. We find the language of the *market-place*. Paul spoke of 'redemption' (*Rom.* 3: 24), a word taken from the world of commerce, even the slave-market, which means to 'purchase', 'buy back', or 'liberate'. This gives us a valuable insight. Christ has paid a purchase price for us.

We find the language of *sacrifice*. The Apostle Paul said (as we continue in Romans 3):

[14] Cited in Sinclair B. Ferguson's, 'Sola Fide' in R. C. Sproul, Jr. (ed.), *After the Darkness, Light* (Phillipsburg, NJ: P&R Publishing, 2003), p. 87.

Whom God displayed publicly as a propitiation in His blood through faith. This was to demonstrate His righteousness because in the forbearance of God He passed over the sins previously committed; for the demonstration, I say, of His righteousness at the present time, that He might be just and the justifier of the one who has faith in Jesus (*Rom.* 3:25–26).

There was 'propitiation in His blood'. Christ's death on the cross was a propitiating sacrifice, that is, a substitutionary sacrifice which satisfied the just wrath of God on our behalf. A holy God, to be consistent with his own nature, must and will punish sin. He will not evade the requirements of his righteous character in forgiving sin.

We also find that the apostle used the language of the *law court*. Earlier we saw that the work of redemption is carried out in such a way that God is seen as 'just' and 'justifier' (*Rom.* 3:26). That is, the cross allows God to both uphold justice and justify sinners. God meets the requirements of his own justice by punishing sin in his Son. Packer writes:

> Paul's thesis is that God justifies sinners on a just ground, namely, that the claims of God's law upon them have been fully satisfied. The law has not been altered, or suspended, or flouted for their justification, but fulfilled – by Jesus Christ acting in their name.[15]

In an historical sense there was a question mark hanging over the character of God. He had 'passed over' or forgiven the 'sins previously committed' by Moses, David, and other Old Testament saints, leaving those sins unpunished. How could he be holy and do this? The answer is, the cross. It was a public 'demonstration' which re-established his righteousness as a Judge, as one who punishes sin without partiality. The sins of Old Testament and New Testament believers alike were punished in Christ and justice was satisfied. Only then could it be said that he is both a 'justifier' (One who forgives sin and declares the believing sinner righteous), and 'just' in doing so. Justice is not compromised because:

[15] J. I. Packer, 'Justification', in Walter A. Elwell (ed.) *Evangelical Dictionary of Theology* (Grand Rapids: Baker House Books, 1984), p. 595.

He made Him who knew no sin to be sin on our behalf, that we might become the righteousness of God in Him (*2 Cor. 5:21*).

A grand transaction took place. He received (became) our sin and guilt. We receive His righteousness, and we receive it by faith alone. Underlying this is our union with Christ, as he suffers as our Substitute, bearing our sin, dying our death. Christ is our Redeemer, our Sacrifice, our Justification.

THE MEANS OF JUSTIFICATION

We have identified the *nature* and *ground* of justification. What is the mechanism by which we receive justification? In other words, by what *means* do we receive it? *The means of our justification is faith.* The means is not doing but believing. There are no religious or moral hoops to jump through in order to be justified. Justification does not come from being good enough, or even of being good enough to merit Christ's righteousness as a reward. What must we do to be forgiven for our sins? We must believe! What must we do to be justified? Believe! We are not saved by keeping the Law or by good works. Faith is only 'an instrument, whereby we lay hold on Christ the Saviour', says the Lutheran Formula of Concord.[16] Faith is the empty hand that receives the gift of God. Hermann Ridderbos, in *Paul: An Outline of His Theology*, described faith as the 'means, instrument, way, foundation, channel by which, along which, or on which man participates in the righteousness of God'. Nowhere, however, is it the 'ground or cause of justification'. He says, 'Faith does not justify because of that which it is in itself, but because of that to which it is directed, in which it rests.'[17] Faith rests in Jesus Christ.

We must not think of faith as a kind of minimalist work. It is not 'the act of believing' that is considered righteous. Rather it is

[16] Schaff, *Creeds*, p. 115. The Formula of Concord is an important Lutheran confessional document written in 1576, summarizing Lutheran beliefs.
[17] Hermann Ridderbos, *Paul: An Outline of His Theology* (Grand Rapids: Eerdmans, 1975), pp. 171–2.

Christ who is righteous and his 'obedience and satisfaction' are imputed to us.[18] Through faith alone we are justified. Yet faith, says Ferguson, is 'non-contributory'. It is 'passive' or 'receptive'.

It has no constructive energy; it is complete reliance on another. It is Christ-directed, not self-directed, and Christ-reliant, not self-reliant. It involves the abandoning, not the congratulating, of self.[19]

There is nothing that we do to earn our justification. We merely receive it by faith and, even then, our faith is a 'gift of God' (*Eph.* 2:8–9). So the apostle asked:

> Where then is boasting? It is excluded. By what kind of law? Of works? No, but by a law of faith. For we maintain that a man is justified by faith apart from works of the Law (*Rom.* 3:27–28).

'Boasting', said the Apostle Paul, is 'excluded'. By what 'law' or 'principle' (NIV) is it excluded? The principle of faith. 'By definition,' Ferguson explains, 'faith excludes even the possibility of boasting.' Faith and grace go hand-in-hand, he points out, 'because of the very nature of faith as a receptor rather than a contributor'. Ferguson continues:

> Faith draws everything from Christ and contributes nothing to Him. Faith is simply a shorthand description of abandoning oneself trustingly to Christ, whom God has made our righteousness.[20]

This is the heart of the gospel. Justification is not a reward for good behaviour. It is not something which we earn for what we do. Paul illustrates this in the life of Abraham, as he continues his presentation of the gospel into the fourth chapter of Romans.

> What then shall we say that Abraham, our forefather according to the flesh, has found? For if Abraham was justified by works, he has something to boast about; but not before God. For what does the Scripture say? 'And Abraham believed God, and it was reckoned to him as righteousness.' Now to the one who works, his wage is not reckoned as a favour, but as what is due. But to the one who does

---

[18] *Westminster Confession of Faith*, X.i.1.
[19] Ferguson, 'Sola Fide', in *After the Darkness*, p. 83. [20] Ibid, p. 84.

not work, but believes in Him who justifies the ungodly, his faith is reckoned as righteousness (*Rom.* 4:1-5).

Could it be stated more clearly? 'But to the one who *does not work* . . .' Stop there! Good works have nothing whatsoever to do with justification. One is forgiven without any reference to works. It is the 'one who does not work, but . . .' – what? If you do not work, then what do you do? Believe! The 'one who does not work, but believes in Him who justifies the ungodly . . .' Stop, again. It is the 'ungodly' who are justified, not the godly, not the one who is doing his best, not the one who goes to church, not the one who is sincere, not the one who is good enough, but the ungodly while still ungodly! We are '*simul justus et peccator*', said Luther, meaning that we are at the same time '*just and sinner*'. The one who 'believes in Him who justifies the ungodly, his faith is reckoned as righteousness.'[21]

THE ELEMENTS OF JUSTIFICATION

When God justifies us in Christ an instantaneous transaction occurs. This transaction has two sides, one involving *subtraction* and one involving *addition*.

The *subtraction* side of the transaction is *forgiveness*. Our guilt is taken away, our 'lawless deeds' are 'forgiven', our 'sins' are 'covered' (*Rom.* 4:7). The gospel message is, 'Christ died for our sins' (*1 Cor.* 15:3). In him we have 'redemption, the forgiveness of sins' (*Col.* 1:14; see also *1 John* 2:1–2).

The *addition* side of justification is *imputation*. Christ's righteousness is 'imputed' or 'reckoned' to us. Abraham's faith was 'reckoned' (*logizomai*) as righteousness (*Rom.* 4:34; see also *Gen.* 15:6). This is a term from the world of accounting. It means to have 'credited' (NIV) to one's account. 'Reckoned' means that the righteousness credited to Abraham 'was not a rewarding of

[21] Rebutting Wright's contention that to be reckoned righteous in Romans 4 is to become a member of the covenant community by faith, Hill says '"Covenant membership" is not the issue of the chapter; being considered righteous before God is, and that because of the problem of sin' (Hill, p. 6).

merit but a free and unmerited decision of divine grace', says Cranfield.[22] This grace is extended even as righteousness is credited to those who believe. Faith, continues Cranfield, is simply 'reliance upon God's promise'.[23] Jesus lived a life of perfect obedience (*Rom.* 5:19). He 'fulfilled all righteousness' (*Matt.* 3:15). He perfectly kept the law. He is the Holy and Righteous One (*Acts* 3:14, *1 Cor.* 1:30).

One further distinction must be made. The theologians have distinguished between Christ's 'active obedience' in living righteously and his 'passive obedience' in suffering the pain and humiliation inflicted upon him on the cross. Of course there was in one sense nothing 'passive' about enduring the cross. Christ chose to suffer and die. No one could take his life from him. He 'laid it down on (his) own initiative' and in obedience to the 'commandment' of his Father (*John* 10:18; 15:12). Yet this distinction between Christ's life and death, between his active and passive obedience, is found in Scripture and does help us to understand the fullness of justification. Through Christ's 'passive obedience' sin and guilt are *subtracted*. We are pardoned, forgiven. Through Christ's 'active obedience' righteousness is *added*, we are reckoned righteous. By his perfect life Christ fulfilled all the obligations of the covenant that Adam failed to fulfil (*Rom.* 5:12–21). In other words, the righteousness imputed is 'the righteousness of the obedience of Christ', says the Formula of Concord.[24] 'Through the obedience of the One the many will be made righteous' (*Rom.* 5:19). 'We are justified not only by the death of Christ,' says R. C. Sproul, 'but also by the life of Christ.'[25] The apostle Paul writes,

> For if while we were enemies, we were reconciled to God through the death of His Son, much more, having been reconciled, we shall be saved by His life (*Rom.* 5:10).

Both the *death* of Christ, by which we are 'reconciled' to God, and the *life* of Christ, by which we are 'saved', contribute to our

---

[22] Cranfield, *Romans*, Vol. I, p. 231.   [23] Ibid., p. 231.
[24] Schaff, *Creeds*, p. 115.   [25] Sproul, *Faith Alone*, p. 104.

salvation. By Christ's death we are rendered 'not guilty'. By
Christ's righteous life, as that righteousness is imputed to us, we
are judged by God to be positively innocent, even righteous. This
is far richer than mere forgiveness. We receive an 'alien righteousness', said the Reformers – Christ's. The gospel reveals what
Cranfield calls 'a righteous status which is God's gift'.[26] Faith
unites us to Christ so that we freely receive his righteousness.

The apostle Paul goes on in Romans 4 to explain this
righteousness, pointing to David's Thirty-Second Psalm:

> Just as David also speaks of the blessing upon the man to whom
> God reckons righteousness apart from works: 'Blessed are those
> whose lawless deeds have been forgiven, and whose sins have been
> covered. Blessed is the man whose sin the Lord will not take into
> account' (_Rom._ 4:6–8).

The 'blessed' man is one 'to whom God reckons righteousness',
and that 'apart from works'. Notice the apostle's point. It is not
as though justification by faith alone were an article of faith taught
in a single obscure place. He points to Abraham and David as
examples of those in whom the addition and subtraction of
justification have been experienced. Their sins were 'forgiven',
'covered' and 'not taken into account', what we have termed the
'subtraction' of justification. They were also 'reckon(ed)
righteous', what we have called the 'addition' of justification. All
this has been done 'apart from works'. These 'case studies' of
Abraham and David are cited as examples of what is true
throughout the whole Old Testament.[27]

> Is this blessing then upon the circumcised, or upon the uncircumcised
> also? For we say, 'Faith was reckoned to Abraham as righteousness'
> (_Rom._ 4:9).

---

[26] Cranfield, _Romans_, Vol. I, p. 100.
[27] The Apostle Paul's point, says Charles Hill, 'is not "being in or out of the
covenant" but "having one's sins forgiven". The emphasis is on getting rid of
the sin problem, not on who's in and who's out of the covenant. In fact, Paul
goes on to make the point that the blessing of faith being reckoned as righteousness was given to Abraham before he received circumcision and before,
incidentally, he was part of the covenant people (cf. Genesis 15:6)' (p. 5).

We are justified through both the pardon of our sins and the imputation of Christ's righteousness. Paul summarizes the lessons of Abraham's justification at the end of Romans 4:

> Therefore also it was reckoned to him as righteousness. Now not for his sake only was it written, that it was reckoned to him, but for our sake also, to whom it will be reckoned, as those who believe in Him who raised Jesus our Lord from the dead, He who was delivered up because of our transgressions, and was raised because of our justification (*Rom.* 4:22-25).

What was recorded of Abraham's 'reckoned' righteousness in the Old Testament was written 'for our sake', that is, for the sake of those who would believe in Jesus.

We have seen that justification is the theme of Romans, the most systematic of the New Testament books. We have worked our way from Romans 1:18 to 4:25, concentrating especially on 3:19–4:9. We can also illustrate the point in Galatians. Arguing against the 'Judaizers', those intent on adding to faith as requirements for salvation such 'works' as circumcision and other ceremonial requirements, the apostle writes:

> Nevertheless knowing that a man is not justified by the works of the Law but through faith in Christ Jesus, even we have believed in Christ Jesus, that we may be justified by faith in Christ, and not by the works of the Law; since by the works of the Law shall no flesh be justified (*Gal.* 2:16).

Notice that he says the same thing negatively and positively six times in this one verse. One is 'not justified by works', 'but through faith' even as 'we have believed', 'that we may be justified by faith in Christ', 'not by the works of the Law', because 'by the works of the Law shall no flesh be justified.' Six times he says the same thing!

Further, he says, 'if righteousness comes through the Law, then Christ died needlessly' (2:21). 'No one is justified by the Law' (3:11). 'Therefore the law had become our tutor to lead us to Christ, that we may be justified by faith' (3:24).

The apostle Paul teaches the same things in his other writings. In Philippians he rehearses his accomplishments under the law, by which he was 'found blameless', but still counts them as 'rubbish' (3:6–8). Why?

> In order that I may gain Christ, and be found in Him, not having a righteousness of my own derived from the Law, but that which is through faith in Christ, the righteousness which comes from God on the basis of faith (*Phil. 3:9*). ✳ ✳ ✳

His righteousness, Paul says, is not 'my own'. Rather it 'comes from God', and does so 'on the basis of faith'.

Finally we can turn to 2 Corinthians 5:21, where Paul writes:

> He made Him who knew no sin to be sin on our behalf, that we might become the righteousness of God in Him (*2 Cor. 5:21*).

Here we see clearly the 'wonderful exchange' of which Luther spoke. Christ takes our sin and was made 'to be sin'. In exchange we become 'the righteousness of God in Him'. Hear Luther's own words:

> This is that mystery which is rich in divine grace to sinners, wherein by a wonderful exchange our sins are no longer ours but Christ's, and the righteousness of Christ is not Christ's but ours. He has emptied himself of his righteousness that he might clothe us with it; and fill us with it; and he has taken our evils upon himself that he might deliver us from them. So that now the righteousness of Christ is ours not only objectively (as they term it) but formally also. It is not only an ontological reality, (there for our benefit in some general sense), but it actually imparts us to the form (that is, the characteristic), of being righteous in God's sight.[28]

The wonder of the exchange could hardly be richer. As Luther explains, Christ 'emptied Himself of His righteousness' (Christ's subtraction) 'that He might clothe us with it; and fill us with it' (our addition). Furthermore, 'He has taken our evils upon

---

[28] Packer, *Honouring the People of God*, p. 225, quoting from Luther's Works, V. 608; from the *Commentary on the Psalms* (1519–21).

Himself' (Christ's addition) 'that He might deliver us from them' (our subtraction). 'Wonderful exchange' indeed!

Not only are we *simul justus et peccator,* but we are also *semper peccator, semper penitens, semper justus* – always a sinner, always penitent, always righteous (or justified).[29]

Let us pause now to summarize our presentation.

Justification is a declaration of one's righteousness in Christ. It is a legal, not a moral change. If I am 'justified' or considered 'not guilty', it is not because I am actually not guilty. Indeed, I am guilty and more guilty every day. No, I am considered 'not guilty' because my sins have been pardoned, the righteousness of Christ has been imputed to me, and God the Judge looks upon Christ's righteousness and not my guilt as he renders his verdict. My faith is *reckoned* or counted as righteousness itself. When God looks at me judicially He sees the very righteousness of the life of Christ. On that basis God renders his verdict, and declares me justified. Again, righteousness is a status that I am given as a gift; it is, says Cranfield, 'man's righteous status which is the result of God's action of justifying', not one which we earn.[30]

Our hymn writers have celebrated justification, both its subtraction (forgiveness) and addition (imputation of righteousness). Augustus Toplady (1740–78), author of 'Rock of Ages', wrote another fabulous hymn which begins as follows:

A debtor to mercy alone,
  Of covenant mercy I sing;
Nor fear, with Thy righteousness on,
  My person and off'ring to bring.
The terrors of law and of God
  With me can have nothing to do;
My Saviour's obedience and blood
  Hide all my transgressions from view.

---

[29] Ibid, p. 225, quoting from *Works,* LVI, pp. 347 and 442.
[30] Cranfield, *Romans,* p. 97.

Notice, 'with Thy righteousness on', or clothed in the righteousness of Christ, he fears not to come with his offering into the presence of God. 'My Saviour's obedience *and* blood', obedience being Christ's active obedience, and 'blood', his passive obedience on the cross, 'hide all my transgressions from view'. His transgressions are hidden 'from view' because negatively, sin has been forgiven and, positively, righteousness has been imputed.

Count Nicolaus von Zinzendorf's (1700–60) 'Jesus, Thy Blood and Righteousness' is also full of the subtraction and addition of justification.

> Jesus, Thy blood and righteousness
> My beauty are, my glorious dress;
> 'Midst flaming worlds, in these arrayed,
> With joy shall I lift up my head.

Notice it is both Jesus' 'blood' (his death), and his 'righteousness' (his life of obedience), that constitutes his 'beauty' and 'glorious dress'. 'In these arrayed', the believer is safe.

> When from the dust of death I rise
> To claim my mansion in the skies,
> Ev'n then shall this be all my plea,
> Jesus hath lived, hath died, for me.

His plea, 'Jesus hath *lived*, hath *died*, for me', references the two sides of justification: Christ's life and death.

> O let the dead now hear thy voice;
> Now bid thy banished ones rejoice;
> Their beauty this, their glorious dress,
> Jesus, thy blood and righteousness.

We are washed clean by the 'blood' of Jesus (subtraction), and robed in his 'righteousness' (addition).

The hymn writers point us to a cause of great joy. Our justification is a rich, full, complete act of God on our behalf. He has not only taken away our guilt, but clothed us in Christ's righteousness. We are 'double-wrapped', we might say, by this double provision, leaving no room for doubt about the adequacy or completeness of God's provision for us. We are saved, completely saved, and cannot but be saved. Luther expressed the practical, psychological importance of understanding the two sides of justification like this:

> You will never find true peace until you find it and keep it in this . . . that Christ takes all your sins upon Himself, and bestows all His righteousness upon you.[31]

Faith

Now let us consider the nature of the faith which justifies. The medieval theologians taught that faith consisted of knowing and believing the gospel. The Reformers agreed.

First, one must *know* (*cognosco*) what the gospel message is.

Second, one must *believe*, or assent (*assentio*), to the message. At this point the medieval theologians stopped, as do many today, erring in thinking that knowing and believing constitutes biblical faith. It does not, as James makes clear in saying, 'the demons also believe, and shudder' (*James 2:19*). The devil himself believes the gospel in the sense that he knows it is true. But faith that stops here is not faith at all. It is 'dead'.

The Reformers agreed with James. Justifying faith 'is not a bare knowledge of the history of Christ', said the authors of the Formula of Concord.[32] One who truly has faith does not merely know the content of the gospel and believe that it is true. There must also be personal trust (*fiducia*), or what we might even call commitment or surrender to Christ. Real faith believes God whenever he speaks and concerning whatever he speaks. But saving faith is not placed in God generically, nor in the church implicitly (see below) but rests upon Christ particularly.[33] It is personal trust or confidence in Christ. It is heartfelt commitment;

---

[31] Quoted in William Childs Robinson, *The Reformation: A Rediscovery of Grace* (Grand Rapids: Eerdmans Publishing Company, 1962), p. 80.
[32] Schaff, *Creeds*, p. 115.
[33] See *Westminster Confession of Faith*, XIV.ii.

94

a casting of oneself upon Christ for pardon and mercy. Jesus used several examples to describe the response of faith. True faith is seen in the one who sells all that he has to buy the field where the treasure is hidden (*Matt.* 13:44); it is seen in the merchant who sold 'everything he had' to purchase the 'pearl of great price' (*Matt.* 13:46). Jesus said to those who would be his disciples,

> If anyone wishes to come after Me, let him deny himself, and take up his cross, and follow Me (*Matt.* 16:24).

The true believer is one who has decisively denied himself, who has fundamentally died to himself. His commitment to Christ is without qualification. It is total and absolute, the 'cross' that he takes up being a symbol of death.

The next two verses show that Jesus is talking about salvation for all believers and not a special category of super-believer or disciple.

> For whoever wishes to save his life shall lose it; but whoever loses his life for My sake shall find it. For what will a man be profited, if he gains the whole world, and forfeits his soul? Or what will a man give in exchange for his soul? (*Matt.* 16:25, 26).

'Whoever' universalizes the application of these verses. The subject at hand is the gaining and losing of one's soul, not greater and lesser degrees of discipleship. Whoever wishes to gain his life must lose it. Faith involves no less because by faith one believes and responds positively to all that Jesus says. Do you believe the gospel of Jesus Christ? That is wonderful! But have you also surrendered to him as Saviour and Lord? Have you 'rolled your soul' upon him, as the Puritans would say? Have you repented of your sins, renounced your idols, and committed yourself to him unconditionally? All this is what is meant by true faith.

Roman Catholic Views

The Reformers' belief that justification was a gift of God through faith apart from works broke sharply with the prevailing Roman Catholic view which came to expression at the Council of Trent

(1545–63). At the heart of the differences between the Reformers and Romanists lay their definitions of faith, grace and justification. Medieval scholasticism defined *faith* as *fides*, credence, or the acceptance of orthodox dogma. It further distinguished 'explicit' faith (belief with understanding) from 'implicit' faith (belief in whatever the church says), even without knowledge or understanding of the content of the church's teaching. Only the latter was said to be necessary for the layman's salvation. Faith for the Roman Catholic was trusting the (Roman Catholic) church as teacher; it was believing all that the church teaches. But as Packer points out, 'A mere docile disposition of this sort is poles apart from the biblical concept of saving faith.'[34] The Reformers said faith is not just *fides* but *fiducia*, personal trust. Biblical faith is trust in Christ as Saviour, not in the church (*Rom.* 3:22, 26).

The theologians of Trent saw *justification* as beginning with the prevenient (or initiating) grace of God. Yet such grace was seen, not as a disposition in the Deity, but a power which enables people to 'convert themselves to their own justification, by freely assenting to and co-operating with that said grace' (6.5).[35] One is justified not because of God's declaration, but because grace (as a power) is 'infused' into the soul and enables one through obedience to become righteous and thereby merit eternal life (6.7; 6.16).[36] For Rome, justification by faith means, in Horton's words, 'sanctification by cooperation with infused grace'.[37]

The Roman Catholic Tridentine (or Council of Trent) definition of justification included, 'not only the remission of sins, but also the sanctification and renewal of the inward man' (6.7).[38] Righteousness was for them not a status but a state. It was not a declaration of righteousness but moral transformation and the condition of righteousness. They believed one is righteous only as one attained and maintained godliness. Those who continued

---

[34] J. I. Packer, 'Faith', in *Evangelical Dictionary of Theology*, 1984, p. 401.
[35] Schaff, *Creeds*, p. 92.   [36] Ibid., pp. 96, 109.
[37] Michael S. Horton, 'The Solas of the Reformation', in Boice (ed.) *Here We Stand*, p. 122.
[38] Schaff, *Creeds*, p. 94.

in obedience to God's commands were said 'by those very works which have been done in God' to have 'fully satisfied the divine law according to the state of this life, and to have truly merited eternal life. . .' (6.15).[39] For the Roman Catholic church to say that grace enables one to merit eternal life, is remarkable in light of what we have seen of the biblical gospel message. Moreover, this fundamental error led to a whole series of subsequent errors. For example, since one could be justified through divinely assisted works, one could also lose one's justification through sin. Then again, what one loses through sin one could gain again through penance. Because grace is a 'power', not a declaration, it can increase or decrease according to one's obedience or disobedience, and especially through the use or neglect of the seven sacraments of the church.

Thus, a system was constructed and defended on the basis of defective definitions of faith, grace, and justification. The whole apparatus became a means of feeding grace (as energy) to the fuel tank of the soul, the burning of this fuel keeping the engine of salvation running, enabling one to merit salvation for oneself. To clarify the distinctives of the Catholic doctrine, Trent pronounced thirty-three curses on dissenting views, including the following:

> If any one saith, that justifying faith is nothing else but confidence in the divine mercy which remits sins for Christ's sake; or that this confidence alone is that whereby we are justified: let him be anathema (Canon XII).[40]

> If any one saith that the justice received is not preserved and also increased before God through good works; but that the said works are merely the fruits and signs of Justification obtained, but not a cause of the increase thereof: let him be anathema (Canon XXIV).[41]

> If any one saith, that the good works of one that is justified are in such manner the gifts of God, that they are not also the good merits of him that is justified; or, that the said justified, by the good works

[39] Ibid., p. 108.   [40] Ibid., p. 113.   [41] Ibid., p. 115.

which he performs through the grace of God and the merit of Jesus Christ, whose living member he is, does not truly merit increase of grace, eternal life, and the attainment of that eternal life . . . let him be anathema (Canon XXXII).[42]

The Council of Trent permanently rigidified the mistaken Roman position. As we have noted, in our century, Vatican II brought many changes into the Church, but a repudiation of the Tridentine doctrines was not among them.[43] Thus, the Church of Rome remains committed to biblical terminology without biblical content:

it misunderstands faith, reducing it to assent;
it misconceives of grace, making it a power rather than God's attitude of favour;
it confuses justification with regeneration and sanctification, making it a process rather than a declaration, a state earned rather than a status conferred.

Packer summarizes the problem in saying:

A society like the Church of Rome, which is committed by its official creed to pervert the doctrine of justification, has sentenced itself to a distorted understanding of salvation at every point.[44]

What do you trust in for your salvation? Are you trusting in the church? Are you trusting that your own goodness will get you through? Do you have a vague, ill-defined faith in a God you do not know? Trust Jesus Christ. He alone, saves. Only by faith in him are we justified.

Further Implications

A number of the implications of this doctrine have, I trust, been made clear. Still there is more to say. There are other practical uses of *sola fide* which must now be mentioned.

[42] Ibid., pp. 117, 118.
[43] See *A Catechism of Christian Doctrine*, Revised Edition (London: Catholic Truth Society, 1985).
[44] J. I. Packer, 'Introductory Essay', in Buchanan, *Justification*, p. 3.

O*BEDIENCE*   (*Excellent Statement*)

First, *justification by faith alone provides the only valid ground* **
for Christian obedience. It has sometimes been said that the
doctrine of *sola fide* breeds passivity and carnality. Those who
claim this fear that it will lead to complacency about the things
of God and a lukewarm commitment to Christ by removing the
motivation for obedience. It does not. True faith always produces
good works. Calvin said, 'We cannot receive righteousness in
Christ without at the same time laying hold of sanctification.'[45]
Those who believe, obey. (John Murray said, 'Justification is by
faith alone, but not by a faith that is alone.'[46]) Faith 'is the alone
instrument of justification,' says the *Westminster Confession of
Faith*, 'yet is not alone in the person justified, but is ever
accompanied with all other saving graces, and is no dead faith,
but worketh by love.'[47] We may say, then, that good works are
necessary, but not *meritorious*. They must follow and flow from
true faith. A faith without works is not true faith but spurious, or
'dead' (*James* 2:17, 26). In the final analysis, asks James,

> What use is it, my brethren, if a man says he has faith, but he has no
> works? Can that faith save him? (*James* 2:14)

'Can *that* faith', that is, a faith that has 'no works', save? No,
because a faith from which no works flow is a counterfeit. It is
not authentic. It is mere assent. The demons have that kind of
'faith', as we have seen. True faith is in this sense 'justified' or
proven by works (*James* 2:21-26). Works demonstrate the
credibility of one's faith. Jesus said, 'If you love me you will keep
my commandments' (*John* 14:15). Remember, the contrast is not
between doing something and doing nothing. The contrast is
between trusting in Christ's righteousness for salvation and
trusting in one's own righteousness. B. B. Warfield wrote,

---

[45] Quoted in Cranfield, p. 95.
[46] John Murray, *Redemption Accomplished and Applied* (London: Banner
of Truth, 1961), p. 131.
[47] *Westminster Confession of Faith*, XI.i.

Justification by Faith does not mean, then, salvation by believing things instead of by doing right. It means pleading the merits of Christ before the throne of grace instead of our own merits.[48]

Faith is not just compatible with good works. It is a necessary requisite. True 'good works' are impossible without faith even as true faith cannot be said to exist unless good works flow from it.

Moreover, *sola fide* establishes the proper ground for Christian obedience because it removes works or merit as a motivation. Obedience must find a higher motive and it does – in love. We obey out of gratitude and love. We keep his commandments out of a desire to please our heavenly Father. The accusation that the doctrines of grace promote carnality plagued the apostle Paul, plagued the Reformers, and plagues those who preach these doctrines today. Our answer is the apostle Paul's – 'May it never be!' (*Rom.* 3:8; 6:1–2). Rather, biblical faith 'works through love' (*Gal.* 5:6). It *works*! Jesus said, 'You shall know them by their fruits' (*Matt.* 7:16–20).

In actual practice, we can safely say that *sola fide* has had the opposite effect to that imagined by its critics. The Reformers were exemplary in moral conduct, as Calvin could point out to Cardinal Sadoleto. Their children and grandchildren, whether the Huguenots, the Puritans, the Covenanters, the early Methodists or today's evangelicals have all been rigorous moralists. Their cultures, whether those of Protestant England, Presbyterian Scotland, Lutheran and Reformed Western Europe, or the smorgasbord Protestantism of North America, have all been beacons of moral light. There is no conflict between outstanding moral conduct and justification by faith alone. Indeed, the evidence shows that justification by faith results in moral conduct of the highest order.

ASSURANCE

Second, *justification by faith alone provides the only safe ground*

---

[48] B. B. Warfield, *Selected Shorter Writings*, Vol. 1 (Philipsburg, NJ: Presbyterian and Reformed Publishing Company, 1980, 1970), p. 284.

for Christian assurance. If justification is a process, one can never be secure because one never quite arrives. If justification is earned, one can never be secure because one never quite does enough. Indeed the Roman church sees assurance as presumption and discourages it. But if justification is a declaration of a God who never changes, it is as secure as God is faithful. Salvation was accomplished in the past, is experienced in the present, and guaranteed in the future. Because it was not earned, it cannot be unearned. Because it was not deserved, it cannot be undeserved. Our justification is a past event (see the Greek aorist in Romans 5:1,9 etc.), anchored in eternity, accomplished at the cross, declared in time, presently possessed, and which cannot be lost. This is the apostle Paul's point in Romans 8. We cannot review it all now, but notice how he placed justification in the middle of an unbroken chain between eternity past and future:

> And whom He predestined, these He also called; and whom He called, these He also justified; and whom He justified, these He also glorified (*Rom. 8:30*)

Then he asked:

> Who will bring a charge against God's elect? God is the one who justifies; who is the one who condemns? Christ Jesus is He who died, yes, rather who was raised, who is at the right hand of God, who also intercedes for us. Who shall separate us from the love of Christ? Shall tribulation, or distress, or persecution, or famine, or nakedness, or peril, or sword? (*Rom. 8:33–35*)

No, no, 'In all these things we overwhelmingly conquer through Him who loved us' (8:37).

While others have seen 'eternal security' as presumption or even as positively harmful, biblical Christianity teaches and affirms it as the birthright of all genuine believers. Having been predestined, justified, adopted, and sanctified, we shall be glorified. What we did not win, we cannot lose. What we did not merit, we cannot forfeit by demerit. Who can calculate the spiritual and psychological good that comes from this affirmation? The gospel tells the weak that in Christ they are strong. It tells the foolish that in Christ they are wise. It tells the fearful that in Christ they are safe. In a world where vows are regularly broken, where commitments are fickle, where everything is subject to change, Christians are anchored to a rock. Because our salvation does not depend on performance for either its inauguration or its continuation, we are secure and 'feel' secure. Even as a child does not earn his father's love but receives it by birthright and is secure in that love, so are we in Christ. 'None shall pluck us from His hand' (*John* 10:28–29). Safe, secure, at peace, rejoicing: justification by faith alone is a liberating and blessed doctrine for the child of God.

As he lay dying, J. Gresham Machen (1881–1937), the great apologist and New Testament scholar of Princeton and Westminster Theological Seminaries, telegraphed his fellow professor John Murray (1898–1975) saying, 'I am so thankful for the active obedience of Christ. No hope without it' (1 January 1937).[49] For years I was puzzled by these last words of Machen. Perhaps others have been puzzled as well. Now we are in a position to understand him. Machen was thinking of the righteousness of the perfect life of Christ that was imputed to him through faith. As death approached he found comfort and hope in Christ's atoning death through which his sins were pardoned (that is, through Christ's 'passive obedience'). But especially precious to him at that moment was the knowledge of Christ's 'active obedience', Christ's righteousness which was imputed to Machen. In the end, our theological details are not impractical abstractions. Rather, they provide the foundation for peace and joy even in the valley of the shadow of death, knowing that we shall stand before God, not naked, but clothed in the righteousness of Christ.

[49] Ned B. Stonehouse, *J. Gresham Machen: A Biographical Memoir* (1954; repr. Carlisle, PA: Banner of Truth Trust, 1987), p. 508.

5

SOLA GRATIA

EPHESIANS 2:1–10

As noted earlier, Luther, in his written response to the great Christian humanist scholar Erasmus entitled *The Bondage of the Will*, called the issue of grace 'the hinge on which all turns'.[1] It is the hinge because, if faith is generated from within, if faith is an exertion of the will for which we can claim credit, then faith is a work, and salvation by grace is overthrown. The Reformers said that, in addition to 'faith alone', we are saved 'by grace alone'. The Reformers saw that to stop at 'faith alone' could have the effect of turning faith into a work. It would be an effortless work, but nevertheless a work, the exercising of which would earn salvation. *Sola fide* and *solo Christo* must rest upon the foundation of *sola gratia*. According to Warfield, 'The centre of the controversy' for Luther, 'lay . . . in the article in which he asserts the sole efficiency of grace in salvation.'[2]

We must also understand the importance of the word 'alone'. Sproul calls it 'a solecism upon which the entire doctrine of justification was erected'.[3] My previously-mentioned seminary classmates who converted to Roman Catholicism have produced

[1] Luther, *The Bondage of the Will*, p. 319; see Chapter 1 of the present work.
[2] B. B. Warfield, *Studies in Theology* (1932; repr. Edinburgh: Banner of Truth, 1988), p. 466.   [3] Sproul, *Faith Alone*, p. 36.

a number of tapes defending their decisions. As one of them explained the Roman Catholic understanding of justification, he pleaded with Protestants to realize that Catholics believe in justification by *grace*, and in justification by *faith*. They just do not believe in salvation by faith and grace *alone*. Christians are justified not by faith alone but by faith *and* works. Grace 'precedes, accompanies and follows' those good works, he explained, citing the language of the Council of Trent (Justification, chapter 16). Grace enables the believer to do the good works by which he may earn eternal life. The believer's good works are not the self-generated works of the flesh condemned by the Scripture, he said, but are Spirit-generated works which are meritorious. Both the Roman Catholic and Protestant theologies are systems of grace, he insisted. Then he pleaded, do not separate from the Church of Rome because of one minor deviation in our understanding of how grace operates. Do not divide over that one word, *sola!* Do not sever the bride of Christ over a highly technical, nuanced theological debate.

Yet sometimes one word makes all the difference in the world. A few years ago I heard part of the debate in the U.S. House of Representatives over federal funding for abortion. One of the Congressmen identified himself as believing in the sanctity of the life of the unborn. But he thought that there ought to be an exception in the case of the 'health' of the mother. Anyone familiar with the abortion debate immediately recognized that his exception was a 'Trojan Horse'. Much was hidden in that one word. The 'health-of-the-mother' language had been used since the 1973 Roe v. Wade Supreme Court decision to permit abortion on demand up to the time of birth. Why? Because it could always be argued that a child may be bad for the mother's health – her psychological health, or social health, or financial health – and be aborted. Because health has been defined so loosely, anyone claiming to be pro-life and at the same time favouring exceptions for the health of the mother may immediately be recognized as pro-abortion after all. One may say 'I believe in the sanctity of unborn life' all day long, but if, in the last moment, one allows the health of the mother to be an exception, one is not pro-life at all. One word determines the whole issue.

The argument at the time of the Reformation, and still today, is not whether one is saved by Christ, faith, and grace. No credible Christian has ever doubted that. The three major branches of Christendom agree – Christ, faith, and grace are necessary for salvation. The argument has always been over the word *alone*. Does Christ *alone* save us by faith *alone*, or do we make a meritorious contribution to our salvation?

In the last chapter we demonstrated the impossibility of our performing sufficient *works* for salvation.

Now it remains for us to demonstrate the impossibility of our exercising sufficient *faith* for salvation. We cannot believe, or repent, or understand, or take even the smallest steps toward God apart from his grace. *Sola gratia* guards the truth that salvation is 'of the LORD' (*Psa.* 37:39; *Jon.* 2:9) from first to last, from top to bottom, from beginning to end. It is utterly 'by His doing' that we are saved in Christ Jesus (*1 Cor.* 1:30).

So what is grace, anyway? The Apostle Paul's letter to the Ephesians will help.

The Favour of God

Grace is the saving favour of God. The Reformers argued that grace is primarily a disposition in God, not as Rome maintained, an infused energy. Grace is first and foremost the determination of God to look upon us with favour and deliver us from our folly. It is 'not something separate from God', explains Williams Childs Robinson. 'It is God Himself in His merciful disposition toward sinful men.'[4]

Children sometimes lack appreciation for a thing done for them because they expect it. They expect a free education, they expect to play on a sports team, they expect to take ballet, they expect

---

[4] William Childs Robinson, *The Reformation: A Rediscovery of Grace*, 1962, p. 3.

fresh orange juice and freshly cut fruit at breakfast, because they have always had them. Periodically I have to remind my children that most people in the world do not have these things, and that I did not have most of them when I was their age. The line, 'We drank *Tang* (powdered orange juice) when I was growing up', may prove tiresome, but it is designed to distinguish rights from privileges, and to stimulate a spirit of gratitude for the benefits enjoyed that are not automatic.

I suspect that the same sort of procedure is profitable for adults as well. It is more than possible for us to take for granted what God's free or unobligated grace has done for unworthy sinners like us. 'Of course God will forgive,' say the presumptuous; 'it's his job.' Regular reminders of the hopelessness of the human condition help us to properly appreciate the magnitude of God's grace. We explored the effects of the Fall at some length in the previous chapter. We may let the Apostle Paul's sobering account of the human condition in which grace finds us in Ephesians 2 take us further:

> And you were dead in your trespasses and sins, in which you formerly walked according to the course of this world, according to the prince of the power of the air, of the spirit that is now working in the sons of disobedience. Among them we too all formerly lived in the lusts of our flesh, indulging in the desires of the flesh and of the mind, and were by nature children of wrath, even as the rest (*Eph.* 2:1–3).

We may note the following:

FIRST, WE ARE DEAD. Grace is God looking with favour upon the spiritually dead. The apostle Paul employs the ultimate metaphor to emphasize our helplessness. We are spiritually 'dead in [our] trespasses and sins' (*Eph.* 2:1). Adam's Fall in the Garden of Eden left him and all his descendants fouled and corrupted by what the theologians have called 'original sin'.[5] Adam committed the original sin, resulting in the deformation of human nature and

---

[5] Chesterton says that original sin 'is the only part of Christian theology which can really be proved' (*Orthodoxy*, p. 15).

condemnation. 'Guilt' and 'corruption' summarize the effects of the Fall of man. How do we experience our fallenness? The corpse is the right image to have in mind when considering our spiritual inability. We have no ability to respond to God. We have no desire to respond to God. We have no capacity or inclination to come to God, obey God, or believe in God. As we saw in the last section, 'no one seeks for God' (*Rom.* 3:11). Look at Paul's assessment of our disinclination to seek God in Romans 8:6–8:

> For the mind set on the flesh is death, but the mind set on the Spirit is life and peace, because the mind set on the flesh is hostile toward God; for it does not subject itself to the law of God, for it is not even able to do so; and those who are in the flesh cannot please God.

This passage has sometimes been interpreted as though it were speaking of two kinds of Christians, the carnal and the spiritual. But actually, it is speaking of believers and unbelievers. The mind set on the flesh is 'death'; 'hostile toward God'; 'not subject' to the law of God and furthermore, 'not even able to do so'; and finally, 'those who are in the flesh cannot please God.' This describes the hopelessness of our situation. The 'flesh' is the Apostle Paul's way of describing fallen human nature. His account is full of the language of inability. We are naturally *'hostile'* toward God. We do not 'subject' ourselves to his law. We are 'not even able' to be subject to God's law. Moreover, we 'cannot please God'. We are spiritually dead.

Other times the Scripture likens our inability to slavery. Jesus said, 'Truly, truly I say to you, everyone who commits sin is a slave to sin' (*John* 8:34; see also *2 Pet.* 2:19). Sin is enslaving. We are in bondage. Moreover, we are blind. 1 Corinthians 2:14 says,

> But a natural man does not accept the things of the Spirit of God; for they are foolishness to him, and he cannot understand them, because they are spiritually appraised.

The 'natural man' – humanity left in its own fallen nature – 'cannot understand' the 'things of the Spirit of God', he says. This is inability.

'It sounds like you are denying free will', one might complain. Indeed we are. We would not for a moment deny human responsibility or human accountability. Nor would we deny that all people are free to do whatever pleases them. But the will is not free. It is bound. On this question Luther was right and Erasmus was wrong. Almost without exception the other major Reformers agreed with Luther: the English Reformers – Tyndale, Cranmer, Ridley, Latimer, Bradford, and Hooper; the Scottish Reformer John Knox; the Continental Reformers – Zwingli, Bucer, Martyr, and Bullinger. Luther taught that one's view of bondage and grace is 'the hinge on which all turns'. An accurate assessment of human depravity is vital if the graciousness of the gospel is to be understood and experienced.

The human condition is graphically illustrated in Ezekiel 37. The Lord takes Ezekiel to a valley full of dry bones and gives him a strange command: 'Prophesy over these bones and say to them, "O dry bones, hear the word of the LORD."' What could be more futile than preaching to dead bones? In the Hebrew, it is emphatic. They were very, very dry. Yet God brought them to life. This is what gospel preaching is all about. It is the proclamation of the Word of God to those who are dead in trespasses and sins and unable to respond. Jesus said, 'No one can come to me unless the Father who sent me draws him' (*John* 6:44). Our situation is hopeless. We cannot believe. We cannot obey. We are dead and in bondage to sin.

SECOND, WE ARE DEFIANT. We are not merely passively unresponsive to God but rebellious against God and his law and all that he would require of us. Our hearts are hardened (*Eph.* 4:18). We indulge the desires of the flesh (*Eph.* 2:3). Ours is not a situation about which one should feel pity. Jesus said, 'You are unwilling to come to me that you might have life' (*John* 5:40). We are willing rebels. John says:

> And this is the judgment, that the light is come into the world, and men loved the darkness rather than the light; for their deeds were evil. For everyone who does evil hates the light, and does not come

to the light, lest his deeds should be exposed (*John* 3:19–20).

Hatred of gospel light is natural to us. We love the darkness. We hate the light. We recoil and turn our heads when the light of the truth shines in our faces. We are both unable and unwilling to please God. Jonathan Edwards, in his brilliant treatise on *The Freedom of the Will*,[6] pointed out that this is how the will can be both enslaved and free. It is enslaved because it is in bondage to evil. But it is free because we always do what is 'pleasing' to us, what we want. We want and therefore choose darkness, we do not want and therefore refuse light. Merrily we skip along the broad road that leads to destruction (*Matt.* 7:13–14). If we want to come to Christ we may. The problem is that apart from God giving us that desire, we will never want to come.

THIRD, WE ARE DOOMED. Grace is God looking with favour upon those who are dead in sin, defiant *and* doomed under God's curse. The self-esteem movement has created a context today where most people seem to feel pretty good about themselves and assume God is pleased with them as well. The apostle Paul says that we are 'by nature', that is, inherently and necessarily, 'children of wrath', born cursed, and under the wrath of God (*Eph.* 2:3). Because of 'original sin', we are born sinners, under condemnation, objects of the wrath of God. From this corruption then proceed trespasses and sins (*Eph.* 2:1), what the Westminster Confession of Faith calls our 'actual transgressions'.[7]

We are in bondage to the world, the devil ('the prince of the power of the air'). We indulge the 'lusts of the flesh' and the 'desires of the flesh and of the mind', be they pride, anger, gluttony, or immorality (*Eph.* 2:3). The civilizing effects of social convention have obscured the hostility against God and his law that seethes in our hearts. The first great commandment, according to Jesus,

[6] Jonathan Edwards, *The Freedom of the Will* in *The Works of Jonathan Edwards, Volume I*, ed. Paul Ramsey (1754; repr. New Haven: Yale University Press, 1957). See also *Works of Jonathan Edwards* (Edinburgh: Banner of Truth, 1974), vol. 1.
[7] *Westminster Confession of Faith*, VI.iv.

is that we should 'love the Lord our God with all our heart, mind, soul, and strength'. We utterly fail to follow this command, preferring instead to love ourselves and our idols. The second great commandment is that we should 'love our neighbour as ourselves'. This, too, we fail to do, preferring a thousand times to love and serve ourselves rather than our neighbour. We are constantly in violation of the two greatest commandments of a God who threatens our destruction for just one violation of even the least of his commandments.

We are all naturally displeasing to God, 'by nature children of wrath'.

Death, defiance and doom summarize the context in which grace is extended to us.

> But God, being rich in mercy, because of His great love with which He loved us, even when we were dead in our transgressions, made us alive together with Christ (by grace you have been saved) (Eph. 2:4–5).

We were everything described in verses 1–3. We were enslaved to sin, indulging in sin and under the wrath of God. 'But God' determined to save us anyway. He took the initiative. Martyn Lloyd-Jones said (in what may have been the greatest sermon of the twentieth-century) we have the whole gospel here in two words – 'But God'. Yes, there is the helplessness and hopelessness of verses 1–3. Yes, we were dead. Yes, we were defiant. Yes, we were doomed. 'But God'! Why did he do it? It was not because he was obligated. Rather, because he is 'rich in mercy'. Because of 'his great love with which he loved us'. How great is this love? Why, it was 'even when we were dead in our transgressions' that he saved us. Even then! He 'made us alive together with Christ'. The apostle Paul underscores the point of it all – 'By grace you have been saved.'

The surprise implicit in the apostle's, 'But God', may only be understood if our death, defiance and doom are grasped. Moreover, what God graciously does, he freely does. He is not under obligation. Why do we say that? Because this is what makes grace, grace. Grace is 'the unmerited goodness or love of God to those who have forfeited it, and are by nature under a sentence of condemnation', says Louis Berkhof (1873–1957), the great Reformed systematic theologian.[8] When God looks with favour upon the spiritually dead, he does so freely and without obligation. God himself declares:

> I will have mercy on whom I will have mercy, and I will have compassion on whom I will have compassion (*Rom.* 9:15).

The apostle Paul summarizes:

> So then He has mercy on whom He desires, and He hardens whom He desires (*Rom.* 9:18).

Grace is God's favour freely extended to the undeserving. We might note that when Satan and his hosts rebelled against God they were cast into hell and no redemptive provision was made for them. God was not required to save them and he chose not to save them. Neither is he obligated to save fallen humanity. Were he required to save, then grace would not be grace – it would not exist. Grace, after all, in order to be grace, must be freely given. Obligated grace is an oxymoron. Obligated grace is merely another term for justice. Justice is that which is morally required. Grace, by definition, is that which is not required but given freely anyway. If God *must* intervene to save us, then he is *obligated* to do so. And if obligated to do so, his intervention becomes a matter of fairness, equity and justice. This, however, is contrary to the whole doctrine of grace. Grace is the unrequired, unobligated, self-determined, self-motivated, freely given mercy of God in Christ.

By now the point should seem fairly obvious. The first step in our salvation was for God to look favourably on those who were not worthy of his favour. This is the background to the great 'but God' statement of Ephesians 2:4–5.

Old fashioned gospel preaching is sometimes accused of being too harsh. Some think that the old preachers harped on too much

---

[8] Louis Berkhof, *Systematic Theology* (London: Banner of Truth, 1958), p. 71.

about sin, the wrath of God and hell.

Perhaps this may have been the case with some. Nevertheless, for the gospel to be true gospel, its darker themes must be clearly presented at some length. We will only understand the greatness of the grace, love and mercy of God when we have understood how unworthy we are to receive it. We are worthy only of his wrath and displeasure. We are incapable of doing anything to escape his curse and death. Yet we received mercy. This is the 'amazing' part of 'amazing grace'. It comes to one who is a 'wretch', and a blind wretch at that! The neglect of the doctrines of judgment robs the gospel of the black backdrop against which the diamond of grace is to be examined and appreciated. It renders us incapable of understanding what John Newton meant in his beloved hymn. Our presumption of God's love for us robs us of true appreciation of his love in Christ.

The whole initiative in our salvation rests with God. We have been doing some biblical and theological weight-lifting. Perhaps we are now in a position to see why. Read the apostle Paul again. He says, 'Even when we were dead in our transgressions, [God] made us alive together with Christ' (*Eph.* 2:5). We were dead. He brought the *dead* to life. Why did he do that? Because of the unfathomable 'riches of grace which he lavished upon us' (*Eph.* 1:7–8). Because in himself he determined to show favour to us. Grace is the disposition of favour in God towards us.

The Provision of God

Grace is *not only the saving favour of God towards us, but also the saving provision of God for us.* Grace, wrote Philip E. Hughes, is the 'undeserved blessing of God freely bestowed on man by God'.[9] As the presentation proceeds in Ephesians 2, grace is seen as a dynamic quality, resulting in divine action to rescue us from destructive sin. Grace, then, is the divine disposition of favour which issues in provision. The apostle Paul introduces Christ and

[9] P. E. Hughes, 'Grace', in Walter A. Elwell, *Evangelical Dictionary of Theology*, 1984, p. 479.

the atonement in verses 5–7. Because God sets his love on us, he provides a Saviour, the Lord Jesus Christ, to save us from our sin. He 'made us alive together with Christ' (*Eph.* 2:5). Further, 'And raised us up with Him, and seated us with Him in the heavenly places, in Christ Jesus, in order that in the ages to come He might show the surpassing riches of His grace in kindness toward us in Christ Jesus' (*Eph.* 2:6–7).

He 'raised us up' with Christ, and seated us in the heavenly places 'in Christ Jesus'. Paul is amazed at the 'surpassing riches of His grace'. Language fails him. All this has been received 'in Christ Jesus'.

The provision part of the gospel story is well known. Jesus Christ was born of a virgin, lived a sinless life, and then died as a propitiatory sacrifice for sin. He was raised from the dead on the third day, has ascended into heaven, and now sits at the right hand of God. This is the gospel. This is John 3:16:

> For God so loved the world, that He gave His only begotten Son, that whoever believes in Him should not perish, but have eternal life.

God *loves,* so he *gives*. The disposition (love) leads to provision (gives), which results in salvation.

Paul summarizes the gospel of grace in many of his letters:

> For all have sinned and fall short of the glory of God, being justified as a gift by His grace through the redemption which is in Christ Jesus; whom God displayed publicly as a propitiation in His blood through faith (*Rom.* 3:23–25a).

As we saw in the last chapter, for three full chapters in Romans the apostle Paul made his case for the universal sinfulness of humanity. 'There is none righteous', he said, 'There is none who seeks for God' (*Rom.* 3:10–11). Then he summarized his whole argument, stating again the universal need of humanity – 'All have sinned', he says. But we are saved ('justified') 'as a gift' and 'by His grace' on the ground of 'the redemption which is in Christ Jesus'. Thus 'grace' is the great motive behind the plan of salvation. We are justified 'as a gift by His grace'. Because God is gracious He provides a Saviour for hopeless and unworthy sinners. We must let this really sink in. The incarnation, the righteous life of Christ (his active obedience), his endurance of the cross (his passive obedience) were all for the sake of hostile, proud, self-righteous, hypocritical, rebellious haters of God. While we continued defiantly to shake our collective fist at God and blaspheme his name, he allowed the whip to scourge the back of his Son, the thorns to be pressed upon his brow, the nails to be driven into his hands and feet, and the spear to be thrust into his side. 'While we were yet sinners, Christ died for us' (*Rom.* 5:8). But more than that:

> For if while we were enemies, we were reconciled to God through the death of His Son, much more, having been reconciled, we shall be saved by His life (*Rom.* 5:10).

Why? Why reconcile and save us? Because of his own inscrutable and gracious reasons.

Grace is what moved the great hymn-writers so profoundly. Hear Isaac Watts again in another of his great hymns, 'How Sweet and Awful is the Place':

> While all our hearts and all our songs
>   Join to admire the feast,
> Each of us cry, with thankful tongues,
>   'Lord, why was I a guest?'
>
> 'Why was I made to hear thy voice,
>   And enter while there's room,
> When thousands make a wretched choice,
>   And rather starve than come?'

Have you ever asked yourself these kinds of questions? 'Lord, why was I a guest?' Given what I am, given my guilt and corruption, given my deceived heart, poisoned tongue and corrupted motives, why me? 'Why was I made to hear thy voice and enter while there's room', when thousands refuse? Why am I not outside with the rest? If you have not asked yourself questions like these, perhaps it is because you have not understood the magnitude of your own unworthiness and the greatness of the grace that overcame it.

It takes great feeling to write a great hymn. Newton, Watts, Wesley – these men felt the gospel very deeply.

Robert Robinson (1735–90) expresses gratitude for grace well in his well-loved hymn, 'Come Thou Fount of Every Blessing':

> O to grace how great a debtor
> Daily I'm constrained to be;
> Let that grace, Lord, like a fetter,
> Bind my wand'ring heart to Thee.
> Prone to wander – Lord, I feel it –
> Prone to leave the God I love;
> Here's my heart, O take and seal it,
> Seal it from Thy courts above.

When I understand something of my unworthiness and the greatness of God's grace then I can see 'how great a debtor daily I'm constrained to be'.

Rightly understood, grace issues in praise. Grace was in the middle of the Apostle Paul's great hymn of praise in the first chapter of Ephesians:

In love He predestined us to adoption as sons through Jesus Christ to Himself, according to the kind intention of His will, to the praise of the glory of His grace, which He freely bestowed on us in the Beloved (*Eph.* 1:4b–6).

We were 'predestined'. Why? 'In love', the Apostle Paul says. We were adopted as sons, he says. Why? Because of his will to do so ('According to the kind intention of His will'). Again, why? All 'to the praise of the glory of His *grace* which He *freely* bestowed [it was not obligated] on us in the Beloved'.

The Power of God

Great as God's provision is through the atonement of Christ, grace does not stop there. Grace is the power of God that applies salvation. Grace is *the favour in God that leads to the exercise of*

His converting power. God did not just provide for the possibility of salvation, He ensures its effectual application on our behalf.

> For by grace you have been saved through faith; and that not of yourselves, it is the gift of God; not as a result of works, that no one should boast (*Eph*. 2:8–9).

How were we saved? By faith in Christ. How did we come to faith? Actually, faith came to us. It was 'not of yourselves'. 'It is the gift of God.' The initiative was all with God. Grace underlies faith. 'By grace you have been saved.' Grace enabled our response of faith. He opened our blind eyes and deaf ears and gave us a heart to receive and believe. We have seen repeatedly that our hymn writers (whatever their theological commitments) often described their experience in a way that is theologically accurate. The Calvinist John Newton (1725–1807) wrote:

> Amazing grace! How sweet the sound
> That saved a wretch like me!
> I once was lost, but now am found;
> Was blind, but now I see.

Notice the passive voice. He was lost, but grace found him. He was blind, but grace made him to see. We expect this of a Calvinist hymn writer. But even the Arminian Charles Wesley wrote,

> Long my imprisoned spirit lay
> Fast bound in sin and nature's night;
> Thine eye diffused a quick'ning ray;
> I woke, the dungeon flamed with light;
> My chains fell off, my heart was free;
> I rose, went forth, and followed Thee.

Note again the passive expressions. All of the initiative is with God. Wesley was 'imprisoned', 'fast bound in sin'. But God 'diffused a quick'ning ray' by which he awoke, saw the light, saw his 'chains' fall off, his heart liberated. What was left to do he did:

> I rose, went forth, and followed Thee.

Faith is a response to grace. Faith is not a work we perform to earn or trigger God's grace. Thus the last hiding place of works is obliterated. How are the dead made alive? 'But God . . . made us alive', the apostle Paul says (*Eph.* 2:4–5). How are the born–again 'born again'? By a decision? By their own will? Jesus said we must be born of the Spirit (*John* 3:5–6). John says believers are born 'not of blood, nor of the will of the flesh, nor of the will of man, but of God' (*John* 1:13). The power of God in grace makes the spiritually dead alive.

Those who deny that works have a part in salvation must also deny any credit for their faith. Our faith is 'not of (our)selves, it is the gift of God'. Our faith arose at God's initiative. It was given to us to believe (*Phil.* 1:29).

I grew up in an ordinary neighbourhood on the outskirts of Long Beach, Southern California. My church was a Bible-preaching church. Every Sunday the gospel was preached and an invitation given. A number of friends of mine also attended the church through junior and senior high school years. We heard the same Sunday School lessons and the same sermons week after week. I came to faith in Christ but they did not. What is the difference between them and me? Was I wiser than they? Did I have more virtue? Was I stronger? Was it because I weighed the evidence and decided? On my knees before God I know, and every believer knows, that the difference between the unbeliever and believer is nothing inherent in us. We are no more wise, moral or sensible than anyone else.

Have we come to Christ? Jesus said, 'No one can come to Me, unless the Father who sent Me draws him . . . no one can come to Me, unless it has been granted him from the Father' (*John* 6:44, 65). Have we 'decided' for Christ? Jesus said, 'You did not choose Me, but I chose you' (*John* 15:16). The Bible says, 'it (salvation) does not depend on the man who wills or the man who runs, but on God who shows mercy' (*Rom.* 9:16). Our decision followed and was enabled by God's prior decision. 'By His doing you are in Christ Jesus', Paul told the Corinthians (*1 Cor.* 1:30). The fact that God initiates and enables our response leads to the humbling conclusion: 'Let him who boasts, boast in the Lord' (*1 Cor.* 1:31).

How does God enable our response? By the working of the Holy Spirit. The Spirit is the agent of application. He regenerates our hearts, works faith in us, resulting in our justification and adoption, sets us forward on the road of sanctification, and preserves us until our glorification. We see this clearly in Titus 3:5–7:

> He saved us, not on the basis of deeds which we have done in righteousness, but according to His mercy, by the washing of regeneration and renewing by the Holy Spirit, whom He poured out upon us richly through Jesus Christ our Saviour, that being justified by His grace we might be made heirs according to the hope of eternal life.

'He saved us,' the apostle Paul says, 'by the working and renewing by the Holy Spirit, whom He poured out upon us richly.' We are 'justified', he says, 'by His grace'.

Now we must understand the steps in our salvation. We do not decide for Christ and thereby receive grace and salvation. It is just the opposite. God graciously chose us and he 'opened our hearts' to receive the gospel by faith (see *Acts* 16:14). The name for God's gracious choice that secures our salvation is *election*. From the mass of fallen humanity God chose to save not all, but many. He made this choice in eternity.

Why are we saved? We can return to the apostle Paul's extended song of praise to God in Ephesians 1 and let him tell us:

> Just as He chose us in Him before the foundation of the world, that we should be holy and blameless before Him. In love He predestined us to adoption as sons through Jesus Christ to Himself, according to the kind intention of His will (*Eph.* 1:4–5).

God elected, or 'chose us', for salvation 'before the foundation of the world' (*Eph.* 1:4). We were 'predestined' for adoption 'through Christ Jesus'. Why? For love. 'In love He predestined us.' In the 'fullness of time' God sent his Son to live a righteous life and die an atoning death (*Gal.* 4:4–5). The Holy Spirit then in time regenerated us, gave us the gift of faith and repentance, on the basis of which we were then justified and adopted into the family of God. Since then the Spirit has been sanctifying and preserving us until one day we will be glorified.

Does the Holy Spirit's work include enabling us to live a life of obedience and good works? Yes, a life of non-meritorious good works is produced by the power of God.

> For we are His workmanship, created in Christ Jesus for good works, which God prepared beforehand, that we should walk in them (*Eph.* 2:10).

We were 'created in Christ Jesus', and our good works were 'prepared beforehand'. All of salvation is of God – Father, Son and Holy Spirit. Redemption is a Trinitarian work, the Father planning salvation and electing a people to be saved, the Son accomplishing salvation through his incarnation, life of obedience and death, the Spirit applying salvation through regeneration, sanctification and preservation. This is grace. The apostle Paul unfolded the 'Golden Chain' in Romans 8:

> For whom He foreknew [that is, us who believe], He also predestined to become conformed to the image of His Son, that He might be the first-born among many brethren; and whom He predestined, these He also called; and whom He called, He also justified; and whom He justified, these He also glorified (*Rom.* 8:29–30).

Election is the family secret of believers. God has done it all. The apostle Paul even uses the past tense – 'predestined', 'called', 'justified', 'glorified' to show that the work of salvation is as good as accomplished by God. Our salvation, from heaven's perspective, is a certainty – certain 'not only before God's people had a being, but before the world had a beginning', as Matthew Henry comments. No room is left for boasting, pride or snobbery on our part. It is all God's work, 'lest any man should boast'.

The biblical understanding of the order of salvation (*ordo salutis*) is as follows:

Election
Regeneration
Union with Christ

Faith and repentance
Justification
Adoption
Sanctification
Perseverance
Glorification

Grace closes the circle of salvation, with God alone receiving the credit for each step in our redemption.[10] The Father elects (*Eph.* 1:3–6). The Son redeems (*Eph.* 1:7). Then the Holy Spirit takes over. The Holy Spirit regenerates us (*John* 3:6), unites us to Christ (*John* 6:44, 65), works the faith and repentance in us by which we are justified (*Eph.* 2:8–9), gives us the Spirit of adoption (*Rom.* 8:14–16), sanctifies us (*Rom.* 8:4–13), preserves us (*Rom.* 8:26–30), and glorifies us (*Rom.* 8:30–39).

Only if grace is complete in this manner is the graciousness of grace preserved. To make this point the apostle Paul cited the example of Jacob and Esau, a clear case of God choosing.

> For though the twins were not yet born, and had not done anything good or bad, in order that God's purpose according to His choice might stand, not because of works, but because of Him who calls, it was said to her, 'The older will serve the younger' (*Rom.* 9:11–12).

Notice what the electing and saving of Jacob prevents. Election makes works-salvation impossible. Jacob was chosen when he was 'not yet born,' before he had 'done anything good or bad', that the choosing principle might be God's 'purpose according to His choice'. This alone determined the distinction between Jacob and Esau, making it impossible to claim merit. Jacob was saved 'not because of works', not because of anything he had done. He was not even born when the choice was made. The God who calls saved him.

Then speaking about the believing remnant of Israel, Paul said that it existed 'according to God's gracious choice', or literally,

[10] For excellent expositions of the *ordo salutis* see John Murray, *Redemption: Accomplished and Applied* and Sinclair B. Ferguson, *The Christian Life* (1981; repr. Edinburgh: Banner of Truth, 1989).

'God's choice of grace' (*Rom.* 11:5). There were believing descendants of Abraham only because of election. But notice what he said next:

> But if it is by grace, it is no longer on the basis of works, otherwise grace is no longer grace (*Rom.* 11:6).

What preserves the graciousness of grace? Election! Predestination! They remove any possibility of human merit, since God chooses, saves and preserves his people.

Response

How are we to respond to what is rightly called 'sovereign grace'? Let me make a suggestion or two.[11]

First, with humble worship and adoration. This is how the apostle Paul responded to the doctrines of predestination and election in Romans 8:28–11:32. When, finally, no more could be said, he burst into praise:

> Oh, the depth of the riches both of the wisdom and knowledge of God! How unsearchable are His judgments and unfathomable His ways! For who has known the mind of the Lord, or who became His counsellor? Or who has first given to Him that it might be paid back to him again? For from Him and through Him and to Him are all things. To Him be the glory forever. Amen. (*Rom.* 11:33–36).

When God shatters the theological boxes in which we have placed him; when we come to realize the full extent to which his grace has planned, executed, and applied redemption, what can we do but bow in reverent worship? The doctrines of grace (as this 'Calvinistic' understanding of the gospel is sometimes called) 'afford matter of praise, reverence, and admiration of God', says the *Westminster Confession of Faith*.[12]

Second, with humble gratitude. Those who understand the grace of God ought to be the most humble of all people. They, of all

---

[11] I have said less than I might have in this section because I have already written a whole book on the subject entitled *When Grace Comes Home* (Fearn, Ross-shire: Christian Focus Publications, 2000, 2003).

[12] *Westminster Confession of Faith*, III.viii.

people, realize that who they are and what they have are due to the gift of God. The apostle Paul's question to the Corinthian believers applies equally to us:

> What do you have that you did not receive? But if you did receive it, why do you boast as if you had not received it? (*1 Cor.* 4:7).

'Who maketh thee to differ?', the old King James Version reads. All that we have is ours only by God's grace.

Third, with dependent living and ministry. Given the extent of our guilt and corruption, given our foolishness, weakness and inability, we above all should live in constant dependence upon Christ. We know our vulnerability.

> Prone to wander – Lord, I feel it –
> Prone to leave the God I love.

Jesus said, 'Apart from me you can do nothing' (*John* 15:5). He is the vine and we are the branches (*John* 15:1–5). Only as we abide in him, that is, as we remain in vital communion with Christ, can we live the Christian life, bear fruit, and be of any use to God. Because of this the Christian life must be a life of prayer, Christian worship must be a service of prayer, and Christian ministry must be bathed in prayer. Jesus said, 'I will build my church' (*Matt.* 16:18). We know that only he can build it. Away then, with our own clever programmes and strategies. Away with the tactics of Madison Avenue, Wall Street and Hollywood. Away with all thoughts of self-sufficiency and self-reliance, and let us live, work and minister in total dependence upon the Spirit of the Christ, who is able to save 'unto the uttermost' (*Heb.* 7:25).

Is the battle-cry of *sola gratia* still relevant? Yes it is! Martin Luther was indeed right. It is the 'hinge on which all turns'. If the doors of self-righteousness are to remain barred; if we are to resist the seductions of the religious systems of merit; if salvation is to remain free to us as God's gift; if God alone is to receive all the glory, then *sola gratia* is as important today as it has ever been.

6

SOLI DEO GLORIA – I

D oes God have a single purpose for which we are to live? Is there a great goal or aim in life? As the apostle Paul draws his theology of redemption to a close in Romans 1–11, he is hardly able to restrain himself. He has developed at length all of the themes that we have discussed in this book: the human condition (*Rom.* 1:18–3:20), *justification by faith alone in Christ alone* (*Rom.* 3:21–8:27), as wrought *by God's initiating grace alone* (*Rom.* 8:28–11:32). Indeed the Book of Romans has been our primary text in establishing these doctrines. The wonder of God's plan overcomes the Apostle: the atonement, justification, faith, love, grace, predestination, adoption, and the work of the Holy Spirit. He erupts in praise:

> Oh, the depth of the riches both of the wisdom and knowledge of God! How unsearchable are His judgments and unfathomable His ways! For who has known the mind of the Lord, or who became His counsellor? Or who has first given to Him that it might be paid back to him again? (*Rom.* 11:33–35).

What is there left to do, he seems to say, but lift one's voice in praise? Then he summarizes:

> For from Him and through Him and to Him are all things (*Rom.* 11:36a).

'All things' are 'from God', 'through God' and 'for God'. He is the source of all that we have. He enables all that we do, and he is the goal of all that we are:

> To Him be the glory forever. Amen (Rom. 11:36b).

Fifteen hundred years later these same verses inspired Martin Luther to rejoice in God's glory and embark on the reformation of the church in order to bring its practices in line with this biblical teaching. Zeal for the glory of God provided the driving energy behind the Protestant programme of reform. Why did the church, its ministry, and its message need to be reformed? Because God was being robbed of his glory. *Soli Deo gloria* became the motto of mottoes.

The Westminster divines spoke with gospel insight when they formulated the first question and answer in their *Shorter Catechism*:

> Q: What is the chief end of man?
> A: Man's chief end is to glorify God, and to enjoy him forever.

God's glory (and the enjoyment of him) is our 'chief end', our chief aim, our purpose in life. The Psalmist cries:

> Not to us, O LORD, not to us, but to Thy name give glory (*Psa.* 115:1).

Non nobis, Domine (Not to us, O Lord) joined the collection of Reformation mottoes. The church must be reformed, they argued, because the honour of God is at stake.

Soli Deo gloria became the motto not just for the church, but for all of life. Johann Sebastian Bach (1685–1750) represented the Protestant tradition well when he signed his musical scores 'S.D.G.', *Soli Deo Gloria*. This was true whether he was writing the 'secular' *Brandenburg Concertos* or the 'religious' *St Matthew Passion*. Just like Bach, we should pursue all *our* work to the glory of God. 'Whether we eat or drink or whatever we do,' says the apostle Paul, 'do all to the glory of God' (*1 Cor.* 10:31).

Biblical Theology

Theology must be reformed 'according to Scripture', as we have seen. If God is to receive the glory, the church must look

to *Scripture alone* for authoritative teaching and not to tradition or clergymen or councils for the content of our faith and practice;

to *Christ alone*, his sacrifice and mediation, and not to the mass, to ceremonies, to priests, or to saints;

to *faith alone* and not to our works, moral or religious;

to *grace alone*, because God is glorified when we recognize that even our faith is a gift and that the whole initiative in our salvation is with God.

Theological reform was necessary because the gospel had been muddied by medieval inventions behind which, in the writings of the apostles, lay the pure gospel.

But reform, then and now, cannot stop merely with theology. The implications of theology push the church forward and demand the reform of its practice. If God is not being glorified in the worship of Christ's church, the government of the church, or the Christian ordering of the family and society, then reform according to the Word of God must take place in these spheres as well. Why? *Soli Deo gloria!* So that God alone will get the glory. God's Word requires that we worship and live to his glory.

Reform of Worship

The Reformers saw that the recovery of the biblical gospel would require a commensurate recovery of biblical worship. In many ways one can consider the Reformation as an argument between the Patristic (that is, the church of the 'Fathers', the church of the first three centuries) and Medieval churches. The Reformers rejected the innovations of the Middle Ages and pressed for a return to the faith and practice of the early church; the Roman Church defended the status quo. But theology drove the reforms. Is *Scripture alone* our final authority? If so, what we do in worship must be determined by God's will as revealed in Scripture. Moreover, if *Christ alone* is received *by faith alone*, and if faith alone is personal trust, then additional changes had to be made. Worship could no longer be merely a matter of the people gazing forward ignorantly at the mystery of the mass while trusting the church implicitly as their teacher.

Luther revised the Latin mass in 1523, deleting the references to Eucharist as sacrifice, and in 1526 produced the *German Mass*. He kept intact the basic structure of the Latin service (less the canon of the mass), retaining even vestments, genuflecting, and a split chancel. But he gave greater prominence to Scripture reading and sermon.

Other Reformers went further. The Swiss Reformer Ulrich Zwingli (1484–1531) wrote his first liturgical work, *An Attack on the Canon of the Mass*, in August 1523. His liturgical revisions began conservatively. But the following summer the churches were 'cleansed' of relics, paintings, and decorations, their walls were whitewashed, and statues, ornaments, and vestments were hauled off. On 12 April 1525 the mass was abolished in Zurich and replaced with a simple, vernacular (as opposed to Latin) service of Scripture reading, preaching, prayer and the sacraments. Martin Bucer's (1491–1551) *Strassburg Liturgy* (1539) and Calvin's *Form of Church Prayer* (1542) reformed the church's worship along similar lines.[1] Reformed Christians have described their governing principle as a 'regulative principle'. This means that worship must be 'according to Scripture'. Consequently worship must be governed by biblical principles and filled with biblical content. All extra-biblical ceremonies and rituals must be eliminated so as not to distract the attention of worshippers from the God-given elements and signs.

First, the Word of God must have the central place in worship. Does faith come by hearing the Word of Christ (*Rom.* 10:17)? Are Christ's disciples 'born again' by the 'living and abiding word of God?' (*1 Pet.* 2:23–25). Are the people of God sanctified by the truth (*John* 17:17)? Are the Scriptures 'profitable for teaching,

---

[1] Bard Thompson, *Liturgies of the Western Church* (New York: New American Library, 1961), pp. 141ff.

reproof, correction, training in righteousness, that the man of God might be adequate, equipped for every good work' (*2 Tim.* 3:16–17)? Indeed all these statements are true. Since they are, Christian worship should be founded on the principle of *sola Scriptura.*

1. *The worship service must be conducted in the vernacular.* It is useless to participate in a worship service conducted in an unknown tongue (*1 Cor.* 14:2–19). 'Grace is mediated through the understanding', said the Reformers. Only if the participants understand what they hear will the prayers, songs and readings be edifying, and edification is a primary goal of worship.

2. *The Bible must be read in the vernacular.* The apostle Paul said:

> Until I come, give attention to the public reading of Scripture, to exhortation and teaching (*1 Tim.* 4:13).

The Protestant liturgies mandated extensive Bible reading, often including selections from the Old Testament, New Testament, Epistles, and Psalms, sometimes as much as a chapter from each. These liturgies turned away from the selective, *lectio selecta* approach to Bible readings to the *lectio continua*, consecutive, sequential readings, similar to that practised in the Patristic Church.

3. *Expository preaching must have a prominent role in worship.* When Ulrich Zwingli, ministering at the Great Minster Church in Zurich, announced on 1 January 1519 his intention to preach through Matthew's Gospel, he established expository preaching as a fundamental pattern, a central principle of Reformed Protestantism.[2] Hughes Old says of expository preaching, 'This has always been the glory of Protestant worship.'[3] The apostle Paul instructed the church:

[2] John Leith, *Introduction to the Reformed Tradition,* p. 34.
[3] Hughes Old, *Worship: that Is Reformed according to Scripture [Guides to the Reformed Tradition]* (Atlanta: John Knox Press, 1984), p. 171

Preach the Word; be ready in season and out of season; reprove, rebuke, exhort, with great patience and instruction (*2 Tim.* 4:2).

The Reformers took the apostle Paul to heart. Luther, Calvin, Knox, Zwingli and other Reformers were all first and foremost preachers of the Word of God.

Second, praise must be biblical and congregational. The priesthood of all believers implies that all of God's people must join in the church's praise. Because believers are all a 'royal priesthood' they must all 'proclaim the excellencies of Him who has called' them (*1 Pet.* 2:9). Worshippers must not be reduced to the status of spectators for a worship service conducted by an elite class of clergy and choirs. Luther should be considered the 'father of congregational song', said Roland Bainton.[4] He restored to the church the singing of praise by the people, which for a thousand years was the preserve of monastic choirs. His first hymn book was produced in 1524. Martin Bucer's *Gesangbuch* appeared in 1541, Calvin's first *Psalter* in 1539 and was completed in 1562.

What should they sing? The Reformation saw a great outpouring of biblical hymns, whether Lutheran chorales, or Calvinistic Psalmody. Our hymn book today continues to reflect this Protestant commitment to rich biblical content in sung praise, that 'the Word of Christ' may 'dwell richly' in us (*Col.* 3:16). The traditional hymn book is a great treasure of music and Scripture-enriched praise which the providence of God has given to the church.

Third, the sacraments must be restored to their biblical simplicity. The administration of the sacraments must reflect the principle of *solo Christo* (by Christ alone). Their administration must be consistent with the finality of Christ's atonement. Hughes Old has abundantly documented how thoroughly baptism had become encumbered by extraneous rituals, movements and words

---

[4] Bainton, p. 344.

that obscured its meaning.[5] Baptisms, for example, began at the church door with exorcisms, the sign of the cross, ceremonial use of salt, exsufflation, exorcism of the water, annointing of the water with oil, the dipping of the Paschal candle into the water, the tracing of the sign of the cross over the water, the anointing of the child with oil, the blessing of the font, and so on.

Similarly the Lord's Supper was obscured by layers of ritual gestures and language driven by medieval theological speculation. The sacraments must have an honoured place in Christian worship. But they are subordinate to the Word and their efficacy depends upon faith. If the sacraments are to edify they must be understood. In order to be understood they must be accompanied with biblical explanation and conducted with biblical simplicity. 'It was because the Reformers prized so highly the divinely given signs that they had such disdain for those signs of merely human intervention which obscured them', said Hughes Old.[6]

1. Baptism was to be conducted simply by pouring water in the name of the Trinity.

2. The Lord's Supper was to be understood as a spiritual meal, not the sacrifice of a physical body; received by faith, not magically *ex opere operato* (that is, by the mere performance of the sacrament itself); offered to the congregation upon a table, not to God upon an altar; administered by a minister wearing a simple gown, not a priest dressed in priestly vestments. The words of institution are to be those found in the Bible, not mysterious words to which are connected exceptional powers. The laity is to receive communion in both kinds, that is, no longer are they to be denied the cup.

Fourth, the work of the Holy Spirit must be given precedence over forms. The externals in worship: the form of words, the

[5] Hughes Old, *The Shaping of the Reformed Baptismal Rites in the Sixteenth Century* (Grand Rapids: Eerdmans, 1992); see also Terry L. Johnson (ed.), *Leading in Worship* (Oak Ridge, Tenn., Covenant Foundation, 1996), pp. 70–1, n. 2.   [6] Ibid., p. 286.

liturgical gestures, the rituals, the ceremonies, the visual displays had become matters of supreme importance to the medieval church. The Reformers redirected attention to the vital thing – the internal, the spiritual, the heart. Jesus said, 'neither in this mountain, nor in Jerusalem, shall you worship the Father' (*John* 4:21). He said to the Samaritan woman that God must be worshipped 'in spirit and in truth' (*John* 4:24). By denying any significance to Jerusalem and its temple, altar, sacrifice, priesthood, and accompanying rituals and holy days, Jesus ushered in a new day with a new emphasis. External and typologically-rich Old Testament worship was being replaced by the spiritual worship of the New Testament. Worship, more than ever, was not a matter of place, time and ceremony, but of the heart, of the spirit and also of the Spirit who enables the true worshipper. For the Reformers this meant that emphasis should be given to the Word which, of course, is directed to the heart. We have seen this emphasis on the Word in our first point. Prayer is an even more overt expression of the church's dependence upon God. 'The Reformation caused a prayer revolution', says Hughes Old.[7] The whole of Protestant worship is absolutely dependent upon the Holy Spirit.

For example, the Genevan liturgy begins with an expression of dependence in its *call to worship* (in other services this is a prayer of praise):

> Our help is in the name of the LORD, who made heaven and earth (*Psa.* 124:8).

The *prayer for illumination* before the reading and preaching of the Word was another such item which the Protestants restored to the church's liturgy. This prayer appeals directly to the Holy Spirit to illuminate the mind so that God's Word could be correctly understood and applied. The emphasis on prayer can be seen also in the restoration of the five-fold *prayer of intercession*. This prayer was a prayer of petition for the church, its ministry, the

---

[7] Class lecture, 26 May, 2004.

lost, the civil government and the afflicted. It had dropped out of the Lord's Day service in the fifth century and was not restored until the Reformation. 'The restoration of the Prayer of Intercession to the ordinary service of the Lord's Day was one of the most valuable liturgical reforms of the sixteenth century', says Hughes Old.[8] They also restored the *prayer of invocation*, the *prayer of confession of sin* and the *benediction*. Worship is a service of prayer because worshippers depend upon the Holy Spirit for both life and worship. 'No one can say Jesus is Lord except by the Holy Spirit', said the apostle Paul (*1 Cor.* 12:3).

The spirituality of worship is closely connected with its simplicity and purity. Simple services were to be conducted in which the Word of God was read, preached, sung and prayed, and in which the 'visible Word' – the sacraments – were administered. This is the pattern indicated by the early summaries of Christian worship in the New Testament:

> And they were continually devoting themselves to the apostles' teaching and to fellowship, to the breaking of bread and to prayer (*Acts* 2:42).

Calvin opposed what he called 'theatrical pomp' and 'theatrical trifles'. He opposed all 'ostentation and chasing after human glory'. 'Calvin's worship', says John Leith, 'is not so much austere as it is economical.' All unnecessary motions, actions, or words were eliminated.[9]

The reform of worship led further to the reform of church furniture and architecture. The architectural focal point became the central pulpit, not the altar. The altar was removed and replaced by a table. Churches, like those of Sir Christopher Wren (1632–1723) – the architect of St Paul's Cathedral in London – were designed to be 'auditoriums', serving the interests of the spoken Word. Elaborate ornamentation gave way to 'plain-style'. All this was done so God alone would be glorified.

[8] Old, *Patristic Roots of Reformed Worship* (Zurich: Theologischer Verlag, 1975), p. 240.   [9] Leith, *Reformed Tradition*, pp. 176–7.

The antidote to the cancerous 'worship wars' of our day is a revival of the principles of the worship of the Reformers. Today's penchant for 'theatrical trifles' – what we call entertainment – might be overcome by a restoration of worship that is simple and spiritual: where the Word is read, preached, and sung in-depth; where the people (not specialists) sing; where the sacraments are administered with biblical economy; where prayer is central; where the heart is addressed and the Holy Spirit is relied upon. Their reforms need to become our reforms once more.

Reform of Church Government

Who is the head of the church? This question has been asked at every Presbyterian ordination exam that I have attended, and reflects Protestantism's traumatic past conflict with the bishop of Rome. Is the Pope (or any human entity) the head of the church? No, Jesus Christ is the Head of the church. He alone rules and commands it. The Reformers denied the antiquity and authority of the papal office. If God is to receive his glory, this must be understood.

How does God exercise his rule? Directly? Through his voice, speaking from heaven? No, indirectly. he rules through men. Which men? Men as individuals or in groups? How is the church to be governed? Luther was happy to retain an episcopal system for the German church. 'He never challenged the office of bishop', says Lutheran theologian Bernhard Lohse.[10] But he did reinterpret its function and authority. He denied apostolic succession, and refused to give to the bishops any peculiar authority. Bishops were seen merely as pastors called to supervise and pastor other pastors. Their tasks were spiritual: preaching, baptizing, comforting, and helping souls.

Reformed Protestants went further. Calvin's *Ecclesiastical Ordinances* (1537) laid the foundation for a more democratic and 'well-ordered' church. What does Scripture require of the church's government?

[10] Bernard Lohse, *Martin Luther's Theology*, p. 296.

First, the church's government is conciliar. This means that the church is to be governed by councils of elders rather than by one man. The apostles were not succeeded by apostles. The apostles were unique. They were men who had been (i) appointed by Jesus himself; (ii) with Christ 'beginning with the baptism of John until the day that He was taken up'; and (iii) witnesses of the resurrection (*Acts* 1:22). There were twelve of them, plus Paul, who is an exception in nearly every respect (he even calls himself 'one untimely born' – *1 Cor.* 15:8), except that he was an eyewitness of Christ ('Am I not an apostle? Have I not seen Jesus our Lord' – *1 Cor.* 9:1). They had unique authority, with the ability to command churches and require their obedience, as is clear in the frequent use of the imperative in the epistles. They had unique gifts of miracles, of 'signs and wonders' (*Acts* 5:12), called 'signs of a true apostle' by the apostle Paul (*2 Cor.* 12:12). They also had no successors. They formed the 'foundation', but not the superstructure (*Eph.* 2:20). 'A succession in the apostleship', said New Testament scholar F. F. Bruce, 'was not envisaged.'[11]

Instead, they appointed elders. Luke writes:

> And when they had appointed elders for them in every church, having prayed with fasting, they commended them to the Lord in whom they had believed (*Acts* 14:23).

Elders (plural) were 'appointed' or 'elected' (*cheirotoneo* has that range of meaning) 'in every church'. Paul tells Titus to 'appoint elders in every city' (*Titus* 1:5). We find 'elders' being addressed in the First Epistle of Peter (*1 Pet.* 1:1 and 5:1–4) which was written to the churches of Pontus, Galatia, Cappadocia, Asia, and Bithynia, being referred to in Revelation (Rev. 4:4, 10; 5:5, 6, 8, etc., addressing the churches of Ephesus, Smyrna, Pergamum, Thyatira, Sardis, Philadelphia, and Laodicea). We find the elders in place in Jerusalem (*Acts* 15:2–4, 23) and Ephesus (*Acts* 20:17–38), and being appointed in Derbe, Lystra, Iconium and Antioch

[11] F. F. Bruce, *New Testament History* (New York: Doubleday), p. 210.

(*Acts* 14:20–23). James, addressing the whole church ('the twelve tribes who are dispersed abroad') assumes the presence of 'elders' who may be called upon for prayer (*James* 1:1; 5:14).

The ongoing work of pastoral care, discipline, teaching and worship were to be the responsibility of councils of elders, not individuals exercising apostolic-type authority. T. M. Lindsay (1843–1914), in his *The Church and the Ministry in the Early Centuries*, summarizes the evidence from the first century saying, 'There is no trace of one man, one pastor, at the head of any community.'[12]

But do we not find bishops in the Bible, too? Yes, and no. Yes, they are in Scripture, and no, they are not there as an office distinct from that of elder (presbyter). Elders were called both bishops (*episcopoi*) and pastors (*poimanate*) in the New Testament. 'Elder' refers to the office they held, 'bishop' (or 'overseer') and 'pastor', refer to their function. For example, Paul sent for the 'elders' of Ephesus and in his address to them said 'the Holy Spirit has made you overseers (bishops) to shepherd (pastor) the church of God' (*Acts* 20:17, 28). Paul charged Titus to 'appoint elders' and then said, 'for the overseer must . . . ' (*Titus* 1:5, 7). Peter exhorted the elders and charged them to act as pastors ('shepherd') and bishops ('exercising oversight') (*1 Pet.* 5:1–2; see also 1 Tim. 3:1–7 and 5:17–19).

The word 'bishop', argues Lindsay, 'is not, during the first century, the technical term of an office-bearer; it is rather the word which described what the office-bearer, i.e., the elder, does'.[13] Jerome (circa AD 345–419), translator of the Latin Vulgate, declared as late as the fourth century that in the apostolic age elders and bishops were the same and, according to Lindsay, 'this idea may almost be said to have prevailed throughout the Middle Ages down to the council of Trent' (mid-1500's), when, 'for the first time, the *institutio divina* of episcopacy became the general

[12] T. M. Lindsay, *The Church and Ministry in the Early Centuries* (London: Hodder and Stoughton, 1903), p. 155.
[13] Ibid., p. 165.

doctrine of the Roman Catholic Church and later, of the Episcopal Church as well.'[14]

Sometimes it has been claimed that episcopacy (the office of the bishop) was universal by the middle of the second-century. This is true, but only in the highly qualified sense described above. The critical question is not what terminology was used, but what was the reality behind the labels? What kind of episcopacy was it? The 'bishop', when distinguished from the other elders in the second century, functioned originally like a pastor among the elders. Every indication is that while the seed of later episcopacy is present, the early church form of government more closely resembles that of present-day Presbyterianism. Church government was, in other words, a representative form of government where pastors were both under the elders and distinguished from them.

Summarizing the sources from the first century which describe the post-apostolic form of government, Lindsay says:

> They prove to us that before the close of the first century bodies of presbyters existed as ruling colleges in Christian congregations over a great part of the Roman Empire. The Epistle of Clement proves this for the Roman Church. The First Epistle of Peter proves it for

[14] Ibid., p. 164. Documents from early church history confirm the above view. The *Epistle of Clement*, dated about AD 95, uses the terms elder and bishop interchangeably just as the New Testament does, attributing oversight to the presbyters. From the second-century, the *Didache* refers to a college of office-bearers who are called 'overseers and deacons'. The *Apostolic Canons* indicate the presence of one bishop or pastor, a session of elders and a body of deacons but, as Lindsay points out, 'the elders rule over the bishop as they rule the congregation, and the bishop is not their president' (p. 171). In the *Letters of Ignatius of Antioch* one finds a bishop, elders and deacons constituting the governing body of the church. His writings are the first to clearly advocate a threefold order of ministry, including a strong 'bishop' who would be responsible for the administration of the sacraments, worship, and doctrine. But the bishop is still complemented by a session of elders; his authority did not extend beyond his own congregation (there was no diocese; it was one bishop per church); and he was not responsible for discipline. Thus, in each of the above documents one finds a plurality of leaders.

Pontus, Galatia, Cappadocia, Asia and Bithynia. The Apocalypse confirms the proof for Ephesus, Smyrna, Pergamus, Thyatira, Sardis, Philadelphia and Laodicea. The Acts of the Apostles adds its confirmation for Ephesus and Jerusalem.[15]

Even at the end of the third century it can be shown, says Lindsay, that 'every Christian community had at its head a single president who is almost always called the bishop', who 'presided over the session of elders, over the body of deacons, and over the congregation', while being subject to the session's authority.[16] Still, Lindsay likens this to Presbyterians 'in the present day'. While the terminology becomes confused, the functions of bishops and elders closely resembled those of teaching elders and ruling elders in the Reformed churches. It is no wonder that Reformed elders should resemble those early church leaders: it was the biblical and Patristic model of church government the Reformers were self-consciously reviving.

Second, the church's government is consensual. Those who rule in the church are called by God, but also govern by the consent of the people. Did the early Christians actually elect their leaders? 'Elect' may be an overstatement, but it does seem clear that the people participated in the selection of their leaders. As we have seen, the word 'had appointed', found in *Acts* 14:23, is the Greek word, *cheirotoneo* (*cheir* = hand; *teino* = stretch out), meaning literally, 'to raise one's hand'. It can mean elect, appoint, choose, and can indicate either 'elect by raising hands' (see 2 *Cor.* 8:19), or appoint or install directly (see *Acts* 10:41). Nineteenth-century biblical-languages scholar, J. A. Alexander of Princeton (1809–60), argued that the verb denotes what Paul and Barnabas did in ordaining or appointing the elders and does not determine 'the mode of election or the form of ordination' (whether by appointment or election). He goes on to say, however, that '*the use of this particular expression, which originally signified the vote of an assembly* (emphasis added), does suffice to justify us in supposing that the method of selection was the same as that

[15] Ibid., p. 163.   [16] Ibid., p. 204.

recorded in [*Acts*] 6:5, 6 where it is explicitly recorded that the people chose the seven and the twelve ordained them.[17] Consensual government is clear in Acts 6:5–6, as Alexander noted. Luke recorded:

> But select from among you, brethren, seven men of good reputation, full of the Spirit and of wisdom, whom we may put in charge of this task. But we will devote ourselves to prayer, and to the ministry of the Word . . . and they chose . . . (*Acts* 6:3–5).

Contemporary New Testament scholar Richard Longenecker says of Acts 14:23 (cited above), 'Here in the Galatian cities the initiative was taken by the apostles in the appointment of elders, *but probably with the concurrence of the congregations* (cf. 6:2–6; 13:2, 3; 15:3–30)'[18] (emphasis added). The precise relation of the people's choosing and the apostles' appointing is difficult to determine. But, with the coming absence of apostles in succeeding generations, the principle seems clear enough – the people are to participate in choosing their leaders.

Third, the church's government is connectional. There was no argument with Rome over the organic, institutional unity of the church. The churches are bound together by a common government, they agreed. The temptation to flee Roman or episcopal tyranny by denying all connectional authority was sometimes strong. But the Reformers avoided the pitfalls of independency because they recognized in Scripture the principle of mutual dependency and submission among the churches. We find evidence of this in Acts 8:14 when the Jerusalem church sent Peter and John to investigate the work in Samaria; in Acts 13:1–3 and 14:27 as missionaries were sent out by the Antioch church and then returned to report.

---

[17] J. A. Alexander, *A Commentary on the Acts of the Apostles, Vol. 2* (Edinburgh: Banner of Truth, 1980), p. 65.
[18] Richard N. Longenecker, 'The Acts of the Apostles', in F. E. Gaebelein, *The Expositor's Bible Commentary* (Grand Rapids: Zondervan Corporation, 1981), p. 439.

But our primary text in establishing connectional authority is Acts 15 and the appeal made by the Antioch church to the elders and apostles in Jerusalem. They met in council and rendered a decision that was binding upon the churches. The basic question to ask is, How could it have been, if the churches were autonomous congregations? The council on that model could only have made recommendations or suggestions that the independent congregations would have been free to follow or not. But this is surely not the self-understanding of the early church. They understood their action to be authoritative and binding upon the churches. The following features bring this out.

1. *The calling of the Council.* Disturbed by teachings of the Judaizers, the church at Antioch sent Paul, Barnabas and others to Jerusalem to seek resolution 'concerning this issue' (*Acts* 15:2). They were asking a higher body to rule on a dispute which they could not resolve. They understood that their congregation was not independent but part of a larger body. There was a system of appeal in place to resolve questions and disputes. If one were to argue that the council was only called at the request of the Antioch church and, therefore, had no authority beyond that granted it by that church, then one, in effect, destroys the necessity of such a council. Could a minority at Antioch have requested the council's action? If not – if, in other words, the council existed only at the whim of the majority at Antioch or any given church – then the council was redundant. The majority in a given church could always enact its own decrees and ignore both its minority and the decision of any council which ruled contrary to the majority. The council would become unnecessary except as a means of buttressing the position of an already dominant majority. It seems more reasonable to assume that both minorities and majorities at local churches could appeal to higher councils, whose decisions would then be authoritative in that church and all the churches. The appeal to Jerusalem and the 'apostles and elders' indicates both a connectional church and the authority of higher church courts over lower courts.

2. *The composition of the Council.* Several factors indicate that the council in Jerusalem was a representative council.

i. The Antioch church sent its representatives; Paul, Barnabas 'and certain others of them' were sent (verse 2).

ii. Elders were involved. We read of the 'apostles and elders' (verses 6 and 23) deciding the issue. Why not just apostles? We surmise that it was for the sake of the future generations. Elders were involved because it was through elders that the ongoing life of the church would be governed. Once the apostles died, elders, as elected representatives of the people, would compose the councils.

iii. The apostles were involved, and thus it was a catholic or universal council.

The basis upon which the decree of the council could be imposed upon the church was not apostolic authority. The decree was enacted by the apostles and elders, but since not all the churches sent representatives, the decision was based on apostolic catholicity. Thus, each church directly involved was represented, and all the churches were represented through the apostles. Marshall says, 'at this stage the Jerusalem church still felt possessed of authority to tell other churches what to do, no doubt because it was led by apostles.'[19] The apostles acted as delegates at-large so the whole church was represented and present at the council. Therefore, what it decided could be authoritative for all the churches. Notice, there was no mention of bishops. As we stated above, when the office of the one functioning as a bishop or overseer is mentioned, he is referred to as an elder. There was no episcopal authority in the early church.

3. *The claims of the Council.* How did the council refer to its decision? It rendered a 'judgment' (from *krino*, to judge, decide, verse 19). It wrote a letter which gave instructions. It sent representatives to communicate the contents of that letter. The Council did not want to place too great a burden upon the

[19] I. Howard Marshall, *The Acts of the Apostles: An Introduction and Commentary* (Grand Rapids, Michigan: Eerdmans, 1989), p. 254.

Gentiles, but it did nevertheless 'lay upon' them a burden (*Acts* 15:28, 29). In *Acts* 16:4 the decisions were called *dogmata*, 'decrees', that had been 'decided' or judged (again *krino*, to judge, decide; also used in 21:25 of the decisions of the Council). John Dick (1764–1833), Scottish pastor and Professor of Theology, said in his *Lectures on the Acts of the Apostles,* that the use of *dogmata* signifies 'that it was not merely advice, or a simple declaration of their judgment, but an authoritative decision, to which the disciples were bound to submit, if they would remain in the fellowship of the church'.[20] The churches were to 'observe' this decision. This was the language of authority with every expectation that the decision would be followed and had become law for the churches (as James indicates in *Acts* 21:25).

4. *The jurisdiction of the Council.* Word was sent to Antioch, but also to the churches in Syria and Cilicia (*Acts* 15:23) and Galatia (16:4). The authority of the decision was recognized in Asia (*Rev.* 2:14, 20), and extra-biblical evidence indicates its application in churches in Gaul. Longenecker argues on the basis of 15:19; 21:25 and 16:4 that the application of the Council's decision was not limited to the few areas mentioned but extended 'to Gentile believers generally'.[21] Likewise, Marshall says, 'The authority of the apostolic council was regarded as binding on churches outside Jerusalem.'[22] Though the decisions were not addressed to other churches, they were applied to them.

So we find in Acts a connectional church. John Dick summarized the evidence in Acts saying:

> The Church in the apostolic age, was not broken down into small parts, detached and independent, but was united, not only by love and a common profession, but by *the external bond of a general government* (emphasis added).[23]

It seemed to the Reformers long ago and it seems to us today that God gave to the church not only a body of doctrine and a

[20] John Dick, *Lectures on the Acts of the Apostles* (New York, 1845), p. 222. [21] Longenecker, p. 451. [22] Marshall, p. 260. [23] Dick, p. 217.

form of worship but a form of government too. That form of government is conciliar. It is consensual. It is also connectional. We see in the New Testament the seeds of the representative or presbyterian form of church government.

THE CHURCH AND ITS GOVERNMENT TODAY

No modern denomination can claim to be exhaustively 'apostolic' in form, but some are more true to apostolic practice than others. A system that is representative rather than hierarchical, conciliar rather than autocratic, and connectional rather than independent, is one which most accurately builds upon apostolic principles.

Why is the form of church government important? Because it is through governmental forms that churches determine their direction, principles, practices, priorities, and to resolve their differences. I am reminded of the words of Winston Churchill regarding democracy. It is the worst form of government – except for all the rest. So it is with church government. Lose balance in one direction and tyranny results. Lose balance in the other direction and anarchy results. Of course, the Spirit must animate the form. But the form itself is God-given, and it is important that we remain faithful to all God-given forms. A consensual and connectional system provides the most efficient, just, and peaceful way for the church to govern itself. Perhaps this is Luke's point in concluding his account of the Jerusalem Council's work saying,

> So the churches were being strengthened in the faith, and were increasing in number daily (*Acts* 16:5).

Having taken us through the debate and the decision, and having told us of the communication of the decision, the net result was that 'the churches were being strengthened in the faith' (there was qualitative growth), 'and were increasing in numbers daily' (there was quantitative growth). When the church handles problems correctly, its ministry need not be disrupted. As E. F. Harrison pointed out, through the decision of the Council, (i) the gospel of grace was protected; (ii) the unity of the church was preserved;

(iii) the mission of the church was enabled to proceed; and (iv) the churches were encouraged.[24] These were no mean accomplishments and, at least to some degree, they were exemplary of what can happen when the church is governed in the way God has ordained.

It is no exaggeration to say that the Christian religion in our day is about to self-destruct because so many have abandoned these biblical and Reformed principles. Too many ministers and churches are accountable to no one. Often there is no council of elders to which the pastor is accountable, or there is no connectional authority (prebystery, synod, assembly, convention) to which the church as a whole is accountable. As difficult as it is to work with sessions, boards, and higher courts, every preacher and church needs just that. Our hero-worshipping culture tends to elevate talented men to heights that mortal flesh cannot bear. One need not be surprised when sexual indiscretions and financial mismanagement follow. Power corrupts. Those who answer to no one inevitably experience the warping of their priorities and personalities, and fall. Since clergy scandal is not an infrequent phenomenon in our day, the collective impact of these indiscretions is all but ruining the Christian witness in our generation. The time has come to restore the principle of rule by a plurality of elders rather than rule by ministerial/priestly autocrats. Similarly it cannot but help to extend the umbrella of accountability over whole congregations and whole denominations. Idiosyncratic local leadership might be tempered if it were made to answer to higher (though democratic) leadership.

If one belongs to an independent congregation one ought to do one's utmost to bind the church to the denomination insofar as this is possible within the terms of the church's constitution. For generations the Independent Presbyterian Church of Savannah, Georgia, has sought to build bridges with the Presbytery wherever it could. Its ministers are members of Presbytery. Its doctrinal

[24] E. F. Harrison, *Interpreting Acts: The Expanding Church* (Grand Rapids, Mich.: Baker Book House, 1986).

standards are those of the Westminster Assembly. Its local government closely resembles that of the *Book of Church Order*. Much of its benevolence money goes to denominational causes. In fact, for years the church advertised the fact 'all its beneficent offerings are distributed' through the General Assembly. The ties are strong and should grow stronger. When new churches are planted by an 'independent' Presbyterian church, it may be wise to launch them with the intention of seeing them become members of Presbytery or denomination. In these ways the tradition of independence is honoured and yet the biblical principle of common government is obeyed as well.

The conciliar, consensual and connectional form of church government will also help to deliver us from the hierarchical tyranny experienced in many sectors of the church. Unelected denominational bureaucrats lord it over lowly congregations. Is not the republicanism of the early church the answer to ecclesiastical oppression?

Church government, or polity, is not irrelevant. Doctrine, ministry, worship and government cannot be separated. Biblical church government provides the 'checks and balances' necessary to keep the church on track and protect it from anarchy on the one side and tyranny on the other. God is glorified when the church orders its government along conciliar, consensual and connectional lines.

7

SOLI DEO GLORIA – 2

The Reformers could not contain their zeal for the glory of God within the walls of the church. Their passion for God's glory flowed out from the church and into the streets, as it were, touching all aspects of life. This can be seen in the family, in culture and in society.

Reform of Family Life

God was to be glorified in the home as well as the church. 'Nothing caught the new clergy up more personally in the Reformation's transition from theory to real life', says Steven Ozment, 'than the institution of marriage.'[25] As was the case with the reform of worship and church government, reforms of family life were theologically driven. The Medieval church held to the monastic ideal of celibacy. Marriage was honoured, but rated below the cloistered life of perpetual virginity. This preference for monastic celibacy arose primarily out of a theological commitment to works-righteousness and an ascetic philosophy of spiritual assent. The result was the demeaning of marriage. Steven Ozment says of the Medieval church that 'by so exalting celibacy and the cloister as the supreme forms of individual and communal

[25] Steven Ozment, *Protestants: The Birth of a Revolution* (New York: Doubleday, 1992), p. 151.

self-realization *it indirectly demeaned marriage and family as an imperfect, second-class estate*[26] (emphasis added). For example, Ignatius Loyola (1491–1556), founder of the Jesuits, urged Catholics in the fourth rule of his *Spiritual Exercises* (1548) 'to praise highly the religious life, virginity, and continence; and also matrimony, but not as highly'.[27] Marriage was seen, says Ozment, as 'an institution best shunned by knowledgeable males'. As for females, 'unmarried virgins and continent widows were always spiritually superior to wives and mothers, and marriage was a debased state in comparison with the life of the cloister.'[28]

When the Reformation affirmed justification by faith alone, in Christ alone through grace alone, it rejected the ascetic ideal and affirmed marriage. Ozment claims that for both the German and Swiss Reformers, 'Clerical marriage was as prominent a tenet as justification by faith.'[29] The Reformers' rejection of the celibate ideal 'was as great a revolution in traditional church teaching and practice as their challenge of the church's dogmas on faith, works, and the sacraments'.[30] 'The Protestant Reformers were . . . the first to set the family unequivocally above the celibate ideal,' continues Ozment, 'and to praise the husband and the housewife over the monk and the nun in principle.'[31]

The critical event in this new view of marriage took place in 1525 when Luther married Katherine von Bora. Katherine, along with nine other recent escapees from a neighbouring convent, arrived in Wittenberg in the Spring of 1523. Luther aided all nine in finding husbands or positions, save one, Katherine. An arranged marriage fell through and a second was refused by Katherine. In the end Luther decided to marry her himself. Ozment suggests she had her eye on Luther from the beginning.[32] 'For heaven's sake, not this one', some of Luther's friends protested.[33] On

---

[26] Steven Ozment, *When Fathers Ruled: Family Life in Reformation Europe* (Cambridge, Massachusetts: Harvard University Press, 1983), p. 12.
[27] Cited in Ozment, *Fathers*, p. 10.   [28] Ibid., p. 9.
[29] Ozment, *Protestants*, p. 151.   [30] Ibid., p. 153.   [31] Ozment, *Fathers*, p. 7.
[32] Ibid., p. 17.   [33] Bainton, p. 288.

27 June 1525 they were married. 'I have made angels laugh and the devils weep', he wrote to Spalatin.[34]

One year later Katherine gave birth to a son, Hans. Luther wrote to a friend, 'My Katherine is fulfilling Genesis 1:28.'[35] Over the next eight years five more children arrived, to give a total of three boys and three girls. They enjoyed over twenty years of marriage. Luther's marriage and family became the ideal which many followed. Home, wife and children came to be seen as positive benefits, not grace-inhibiting burdens.

The Reformers brought a number of new ideals to marriage.

First, they esteemed marriage as companionship. Luther depended upon Katherine as his companion, helper and friend. When she was ill he cried, 'Oh, Katie, do not die and leave me.'[36] He paid her the highest compliments, calling the book of Galatians (his favourite) 'my Katherine von Bora'. He said of her,

> My Katie is in all things so obliging and pleasing to me that I would not exchange my poverty for the riches of Croesus.[37]

He spoke with the voice of an experienced husband when he said, 'There is no bond on earth so sweet nor any separation so bitter as that which occurs in a good marriage.'[38] The classical ideal of companionship among male friends was transferred by the Reformers and their successors to marriage. One's wife was to be one's closest and dearest friend. One hundred and fifty years after Luther, Matthew Henry, commenting on Genesis 2:22, spoke for the whole Reformation tradition when he said:

> The woman was *made of a rib out of the side of Adam*; not made out of his head to top him, nor out of his feet to be trampled upon by him, but out of his side to be equal with him, under his arm to be protected, and near his heart to be beloved.[39]

Men came to see their wives as co-workers and equals, if still subordinate. Husbands and wives worked together to build the

---

[34] Ibid., p. 289. [35] Ibid., p. 293. [36] Ibid., p. 302. [37] Ibid., p. 293.
[38] Ozment, *Protestants*, p. 160.
[39] Matthew Henry, *Commentary on the Whole Bible* (many editions).

family and raise the children. The Reformers encouraged the education of girls so that they might read the Bible for themselves and better nurture the children in the Christian faith. Husbands and wives were partners. Calvin expressed this attitude in his tribute to his wife upon her death:

> I have been bereaved of the best companion of my life, of one who, had it been so ordered, would not only have been the willing share of my indigence, but even of my death. During her life she was the faithful helper of my ministry.[40]

Second, they esteemed sexual relations within marriage. The dominant view arising out of the Middle Ages was that sexual desire was evil, even in marriage. Virginity and celibacy were glorified. Augustine portrayed the marriage act in Paradise as occurring without passion. Even married couples were encouraged to abstain. This was all part of the prevailing neo-Platonic spirituality which saw spiritual progress occurring through the suppression of bodily appetites. Fasting, celibacy, even denying the body sleep were seen as necessary disciplines for the serious Christian. The Church Fathers were nearly unanimous in affirming asceticism and specifically in affirming celibacy. Luther criticized the older theologians (Jerome, Cyprian, Augustine and Gregory) for 'never having written anything good about marriage'.[41] In opposing this view the Reformers affirmed the goodness of sexual relations and even sexual pleasure in marriage. Medieval society regrettably had become polarized between the celibate ideal and the celebration of adulterous romantic love in the love stories and poems of the era. But as Leland Ryken points out, the Reformation altered the equation:

> By the time we reach the end of the sixteenth century, the ideal of

---

[40] Donald Kagan, Steven Ozment, Frank M. Turner, *The Western Heritage,* 7th Edition (Upper Saddle River, N.J.: Prentice Hall, 2001), p. 380; quoting J. Bonnet, trans., *Letters of John Calvin*, Vol. 2. (Edinburgh: T. Constable, 1858), p. 216.

[41] Quoted in Ozment, *Protestants*, p. 152.

wedded romantic love had replaced the adulterous courtly love ideal of the Middle Ages as the customary subject for literature.[42]

Ryken quotes C. S. Lewis, who argued that

The conversion of courtly love into romantic monogamous love was . . . largely the work of English, and even of Puritan, poets.[43]

Similarly Herbert Richardson, another modern scholar cited by Ryken, claims that the Puritans

did what courtly lovers had never dared to do: by combining the romantic love relation and the marriage relation, they created the new social institution of romantic marriage.[44]

Further he says:

The rise of romantic marriage and its validation by the Puritans . . . represents a major innovation within the Christian tradition.[45]

Third, they esteemed children and the task of child rearing. Luther was a vigorous defender of marriage and parenting. According to Ozment, 'He exalted the family in all its dimensions and utterly without qualification.'[46] Against the Medieval tendency to either denigrate women as temptresses (like Eve) or exalt them as virgins (like Mary), the Reformers praised their divine vocation as wives and mothers. 'There is no power on earth that is nobler or greater than that of parents', said Luther.[47] The greatest service that one could perform for humanity was to rear godly children. 'When a father washes diapers or performs some other mean task for his child,' said Luther, 'God with all His angels and creatures is smiling.'[48]

The new Protestant family was seen, not as a necessary concession to weakness, nor as a grace-inhibiting burden, but as the foundation of society. Fathers were seen as priests, families as 'little churches', the home as 'the cradle of civilization'. Child rearing

---

[42] Leland Ryken, *Worldly Saints: The Puritans as They Really Were* (Grand Rapids: Zondervan, 1986), p. 51.   [43] Ibid., p. 51.   [44] Ibid., p. 51.
[45] Ibid., p. 234, note 81.   [46] Ozment, *Protestants*, p. 165.
[47] Ozment, *Fathers*, p. 132.   [48] Ibid., p. 8.

was understood as more than nutrition and hygiene. The spiritual welfare of the children was at the centre of the family's concerns. During the Middle Ages the monasteries were communities of prayer. Wherever the Reformation took root, the responsibility for daily prayer shifted to the Christian home. Family worship in the home became a hallmark of Protestantism for generations and right up until the recent past. Few practices of our forefathers are in more need of reviving today than this.[49]

Marriage, says Ozment, was viewed as 'the foundation and nucleus of society and the divine instrument for its stability and reform'. Management of the household was seen 'as the highest human art'.[50] J. I. Packer credits the English Puritans with virtually creating the family as we have come to know of it in the English speaking world, saying '. . . in the same sense in which, under God, they were creators of the English Christian Sunday, so they were creators of the English Christian marriage, the English Christian family, and the English Christian home.'[51]

A strong infusion of these biblical views of marriage, children and family could not but help in a world where cohabitation, illegitimacy and divorce have become commonplace, and where the family may be on the verge of collapse. The Christian home, reconstituted and reinvigorated according to these biblical and traditional lines may be the Christian community's clearest witness at the beginning of the 21st century – our light in the darkness of familial distress, our city set upon a hill.

Reform of Culture and Society

Human cultural activities are also to be pursued to the glory of God, taught the Reformers. Behind this idea lay the convictions of (i) the goodness of creation; (ii) the goodness of all legitimate

---

[49] See Terry L. Johnson, *The Family Worship Book* (Fearn, Ross-shire: Christian Focus Publications, 1998, 2003).
[50] Ozment, *Fathers*, p. 9.
[51] J. I. Packer, 'Marriage and Family in Puritan Thought', in *A Quest for Godliness* (Wheaton: Crossway Books, 1990), p. 260.

vocations within the creation. They would not accept a dichotomy between the gospel and the world, the church and culture. God created the world and called it good. 'The Reformation idea of calling', says Robert Knudsen, 'leads to the idea that sanctity attaches to what are broadly called man's "cultural activities".'[52] Artists, educators, tradesmen, entrepreneurs, and magistrates were alike released to pursue their callings in their appointed and chosen sphere to the glory of God. This had powerful implications for the development of much that is good in the modern world.

EDUCATION

Since one is justified by faith, and since this faith is a personal judgment made in light of one's understanding of the Bible, literacy was indispensable in Protestant cultures. 'Literacy is an optional concern for some forms of piety,' says John Leith, 'but for Protestants it is a virtual necessity.'[53] Bainton claimed that

> one can without exaggeration ascribe to the Reformation the creation of the first body of religious literature for the young.[54]

As early as 1523 Luther began to advocate for a universal and compulsory system of education. 'The Scripture cannot be understood without the languages, the languages can be learned only in school', said Luther.[55] Luther also developed a children's catechism, his 'Small Catechism' for the instruction of the young.

The Reformers cherished not only religious education but all learning. Melanchthon revised the curriculum at the University of Wittenberg, eliminating aspects of the medieval scholasticism and broadening the humanistic base, including history, poetry, classical languages, Hebrew and mathematics. Calvin displayed 'a love for the liberal arts', and viewed the natural sciences as 'gifts of God', says Knudsen. Leith writes:

[52] Robert Knudsen, 'Calvinism as a Cultural Force', in W. Stanford Reid (ed.), *John Calvin: His Influence in the Western World* (Grand Rapids: Zondervan, 1982), p. 23.　[53] Leith, *Reformed Tradition*, p. 220.
[54] Bainton, p. 336.　[55] Bainton, p. 335.

John Calvin emphasized the importance of learning not merely in order to study the Bible but also *in order to study God's created order* (emphasis added).[56]

Leith continues, 'The study of the liberal arts was for him an act of Christian obedience.'[57] Calvin founded the Geneva Academy in 1559, attracting students from all over the world. The Academy later developed into the University of Geneva, which today is recognized as one of the world's great universities. John Knox said of Calvin's Geneva that it was 'the most perfect school of Christ since the time of the apostles'.

Concern for broad-based education has been a hallmark of Protestantism, and especially Reformed Protestantism, wherever it has gone. We may take the Puritans as an example. When they established their 'Holy Commonwealth' in New England, they quickly made provision for education. In 1635 (just five years after the founding of the colony) they established the Boston Latin School for the education of young boys. The next year Harvard College was founded for the training of ministers. This story is instructive of the outlook of the Reformers, as their programme of reform was carried on by succeeding generations.

The Rev. John Harvard (1607–38) came to the Massachusetts Bay Colony in 1635 and died shortly thereafter. His will left behind £750 and 400 books for the establishment of a college for the training of ministers in New England. The college was established on the Charles River at New Town, and in 1636 was named after John Harvard, while the location was renamed Cambridge after the college at which so many of the Puritan ministers had been educated. The need for a 'learned ministry' was expressed in the book *New England's First Fruits* (1643), in the following memorable words,

> After God had carried us safe to New England, and we had builded our houses, provided necessaries for our livelihood, reared convenient places for God's worship, and settled the civil government; one of the next things we longed for, and looked after

[56] Leith, p. 220.   [57] Ibid.

was to advance learning and perpetuate to Posterity; dreading to leave an illiterate ministry to the churches, when our present ministers shall lie in the dust.[58]

The original motto of the college was *Veritas Christo et Ecclesiae*, Truth for Christ and the Church.

The New England Puritans believed in educating everyone, not just ministers. In 1647 they provided for compulsory universal learning, adopting the 'Old Deluder Satan Act', as it became known. This act called for the formation of mandatory common schools. Towns of 50 or more families were required to hire an instructor to teach reading and writing. Towns of 100 or more families were required to establish grammar schools. The purpose was to promote literacy in order to equip the populace for spiritual warfare. The Act reasoned:

> It being one huge project of that old deluder Satan to keep men from the knowledge of the Scriptures, as in former times by keeping them in an unknown tongue, so in these latter times by persuading from the use of tongues, that so at least the true sense and meaning of the original might be clouded by false glosses of saint-seeming deceivers, that learning may not be buried in the grave of our fathers in the church and commonwealth, the Lord assisting our endeavors: It is therefore ordered that every township in this jurisdiction . . .[59]

New England Puritans produced the *New England Primer* in 1687, the first textbook published in North America. It was loaded with biblical content, including The Lord's Prayer, the Apostles' Creed, portions of the *Shorter Catechism*, and Bible verses. For example, it taught the alphabet through short poems with Bible references.

A – In Adam's fall we sinned all.

B – Having to find the Bible mind.

C – Christ crucified for sinners died.

D – the Deluge drowned the earth around.

[58] Sydney Ahlstrom, *A Religious History of the American People* (New Haven: Yale University Press, 1972), p. 149.
[59] Mortimer J. Adler (ed). *The Annals of America*, Vol. 1 (Chicago: Encylopaedia Britannica, Inc., 1968), p. 184.

Neil Postman, in his book *Amusing Ourselves to Death*, notes: 'Between 1640 and 1700, the literacy rate for men in Massachusetts and Connecticut was somewhere between 89% and 95%, quite probably the highest concentration of literate males to be found anywhere in the world at that time. (The literacy rate for women in those colonies is estimated to have run as high as 62% in the years 1681 to 1697).'[60]

Postman found a surprising variety of books, religious and non-religious, and an amazing quantity of books, being bought and sold in New England, a testimony to the esteem with which the Puritans held all learning. Leith reports that prior to the Civil War the Reformed churches founded 75 colleges (Presbyterians – 49; Congregationalists – 21; German Reformed – 4; Dutch Reformed – 1), a 'notable' accomplishment, he says, 'in the light of the minimal financial resources that were available'.[61] The Reformation was the best friend that education ever had. Learning is a good thing, the Protestant tradition continues to say, to be pursued to the glory of God.

POLITICAL ORDER

In *The Freedom of the Christian Man* (1520), Luther described the gospel-liberated Christian as being a 'lord over all and subject to none'.[62] Though this was applied by Luther to the doctrine of salvation (soteriology), it had implications in the political and economic realms as well. Neither Luther nor Calvin worked through the political implications of their theology, but their successors did. If God is to receive his glory, his truth must be applied to the political realm as well as the ecclesiastical, familial, and educational. Among the political principles to come out of the Reformation were the following:

The freedom of the church from state control.

---

[60] Postman, *Amusing Ourselves to Death* (New York: Penguin Books, 1985), p. 32.   [61] Leith, p. 220.
[62] Ozment, *Protestants*, p. 142.

The right of resistance to tyrants, particularly through the orderly opposition of the lower magistrates.[63]

The equality of all men under the rule of God, in sin and in grace.

The right of private judgment and freedom of conscience.

Consensual government in the church.

These principles ultimately had an impact on the political realm. Calvin argued for a 'two-powers' view of the church and state. There are, he said, two independent realms, each ordained by God, each legitimate in its own right and free from the control of the other. This meant that the power of the state was necessarily *limited*. This meant that a tyrant who overstepped his bounds might be *resisted*. The *equality* of all men (under God, in sin, and in grace), and the right of each church member, regardless of class, race or wealth to *vote* in the selection of their leaders, gave impetus to *democratic forms* in the civil government. The right of *private judgment* and *freedom of conscience* became the anvil upon which religious toleration and religious liberty were wrought, and ultimately, with them, the freedoms of speech, assembly and of the press were won. Finally, the doctrine of depravity (equality in sin) meant that power could not be entrusted to one or a few, but must be spread out, diffused, and separated, with multiple 'checks and balances' upon each power wielding entity.

The shock troops in the battle for representative democracy and fundamental human rights were England's and New England's Puritans, France's Huguenots, Holland's 'Beggars', and Scotland's Covenanters. In particular the Puritans fought for over a hundred years for religious liberty, not winning toleration until 1688. They worked out their positive views of government in the Long Parliament (1640–52), in Cromwell's Commonwealth (1651–60) and especially in New England (1630 onwards).

They were advocates of limited government. John Cotton (1584–1652), a founding pastor of the New England colony, said:

[63] See Calvin, *Institutes*, IV.xx.31.

Let all the world learn to give mortal men no greater power than they are content they shall use, for use it they will . . . It is necessary therefore, that all power that is on earth be limited.

They were advocates of the rule of law, of government defined by covenant and constitution, not left to the arbitrary whims of men.

They were advocates of rule with the consent of the governed. The 'Pilgrim Code of Law' of 1636, the Massachusetts 'Body of Liberties' of 1641, and the 'Fundamental Orders of Connecticut' of 1639 all appeal to the consent of the governed as a fundamental right, long before John Locke began to write.

They were advocates of representative government. Although the Puritans of New England established a limited franchise (male church members only, or from one-quarter to one-half of the male population of the colonies), public officials were elected by the people from the very beginning in New England.

They were advocates of the separation of powers. This was an important aspect of the 'New England Way', articulated in the writings of John Cotton, Thomas Hooker (1586–1647), Thomas Shepard (1605–49), John Davenport (1597–1670) and Richard Mather (1596–1669). The Puritans established 'Bible Common-wealths', yet believed that the church and state had separate jurisdictions. The clergy did not wield political power. The state was not a theocracy and, according to the great Yale historian Sydney Ahlstrom (1919–84), to call it such is 'absurd'. Ahlstrom cites with approval Harvard historian Perry Miller's (1905–63) statement that 'of all the governments in the western world at that time that of early Massachusetts gave the clergy least authority'.[64] Yet the civil magistrates did punish violations of the Ten Commandments, heresy, blasphemy, idolatry, Sabbath breaking, trouble making and so on.[65]

---

[64] Ahlstrom, *Religious History of the American People*, p. 147.
[65] The Cambridge Platform of 1648 called on the civil government to enforce orthodoxy. 'Idolatry, blasphemy, heresy, venting corrupt and pernicious opinions, that destroy the foundation, open contempt of the word preached,

Of course this meant the Puritans did not promote religious freedom as we understand it. Indeed they persecuted the Quakers and other sects. Nathaniel Ward, who came to Massachusetts Bay in 1634 and became pastor of Ipswich, wrote a tract he entitled *The Simple Cobbler of Aggawam in America*, and boldly asserted:

> I dare take it upon me to be the herald of New England so far as to proclaim to the world, in the name of our colony, that all Familists, Antinomians, Anabaptists and other enthusiasts shall have free liberty to keep away from us; and such as will come, to be gone as fast as they can, the sooner the better . . . I dare aver that God does nowhere in his word tolerate Christian states to give toleration to such adversaries of his truth, if they have power in their hands to suppress them.[66]

They asserted the right of resistance to tyrants. Calvin's *Institutes* asserted the right of resistance to the 'fierce licentiousness of kings' through lesser magistrates (in the last edition [1559], though the teaching is substantially the same in the 1536 edition). Even individuals may resist tyranny. The Puritans concurred, and through Parliament resisted the Stuart monarchy in Great Britain; and their children in New England, a century later, resisted the British monarchy in America. Paul Johnson said, 'In a sense, the United States was a posthumous child of the Long Parliament.'[67]

---

profanation of the Lord's Day, disturbing the peaceable administration and exercise of the worship and holy things of God, and the like, are to be restrained, and punished by civil authority.' The civil authorities could call a synod, but the composition of the synod was seen as a matter for the church. Though separate, church and state were seen as working together. Again, according to the Cambridge Platform of 1648, 'Church government stands in no opposition to civil government of commonwealths . . . whereas the contrary is most true, that they may both stand together and flourish and the one being helpful unto the other, in a distinct and new administrations . . .' (*Annals of America*, Vol. 1, p. 194).

[66] Paul A. Johnson, *A History of the American People* (New York: Harper Collins, 1997) p. 41.   [67] Ibid., p. 147.

Many of the same principles surfaced in the development of the Dutch Republic, under the influence of Dutch Calvinism, a few years earlier than in the English-speaking world.[68]

The impact of the Reformation on the political realm has been profound. The rights and freedoms that we enjoy today are, to a large extent, God's gift to us through the Reformers and their successors.[69]

ECONOMICS

Does the idea of the 'freedom of the Christian man' have any implications in the economic realm? We would expect that it would. Political freedom implies economic freedom, that is, the freedom to make choices in the buying and selling of goods and services. God is to be glorified in the workplace as well as in the place of prayer; Christian people must make their economic decisions to the glory of God. The Reformation, and in particular Reformed Protestantism, played a significant role in the development of free markets, as several powerful ideas came together at one time.

1. *Basic human rights.* As we have seen, the right of private judgment and liberty of conscience demanded by Protestants laid the foundation not only for the basic human rights of speech, press and assembly, but also the right to make basic economic choices.

2. *The doctrine of vocation.* Each person was said to have his or her calling from God, to be pursued to the glory of God. This was one of the many insights flowing from the doctrine of the priesthood of all believers. Paul Marshall summarizes the impact of the new outlook: 'It was through the idea of calling that

[68] Abraham Kuyper argues this in his *Lectures on Calvinism* (Grand Rapids: Wm. B. Eerdmans, 1931, 1983).
[69] For a brilliant survey of the evidence for this view see Douglas Kelly, *The Emergence of Liberty in the Modern World: The Influence of Calvin on Five Governments from the 16th through 18th Centuries* (Phillipsburg, N. J.: Presbyterian & Reformed,1992).

everyday work acquired religious significance. The peasant and the merchant came to be seen as doing God's work as much as the nun, the priest, and the magistrate.'[70]

3. *The dignity of labour.* This is closely associated with the preceding point. All legitimate work was seen as God's work and good. Because the Reformers denied the distinction between clergy and laity, they also denied the distinction between sacred and secular work. The superiority of a 'religious' vocation was denied, the legitimacy of a 'secular' vocation was affirmed. Life in the work-world was no longer a lesser kind of life, as it had been with Augustine (354–430) and Aquinas (1225–74). 'With Luther there came a different world', says Paul Marshall. 'The workshop was a sphere of the highest Christian service.'[71]

4. *The emphasis upon a well-ordered, disciplined, simple life.* 'Well-ordered' meant that all of life's tasks could receive their proper attention. 'Disciplined' meant that work was undertaken with diligence. 'Simple life' meant that life was lived without ostentation or excess, and so resources were conserved and capital accumulated.

History is complex and many factors come into play on the development of any given movement. Nevertheless as Leith summarizes the evidence, 'Reformed theology and ethics have been an important ingredient in shaping the lives of the persons and communities that have been identified with the development of capitalism'.[72] It has been no accident that those nations where

---

[70] Paul Marshall, *A Kind of Life Imposed on Man: Vocation & Social Order from Tyndale to Locke* (Toronto, Buffalo, London: University of Toronto Press, 1996), p. 97.

[71] Ibid., p. 3.   [72] Leith, p. 218. See in addition to works already cited John T. McNeill, *The History and Character of Calvinism* (New York: Oxford University Press, 1954). For a more recent study which sees Protestantism's distinctives as circumstantial rather than central in the development of freedom and prosperity, see Philip Benedict, *Christ's Churches Purely Reformed: A Social History of Calvinism* (New Haven and London: Yale University Press, 2002). On the other hand, the highly-regarded historian Samuel P. Huntington, in his *Who Are We?* (New York: Simon & Schuster,

the Reformation has had the greatest influence (the United States, Great Britain, Germany, Holland, Scandinavia) have experienced the greatest economic growth and prosperity.

THE ARTS

The accusation has often been hurled at Protestants, particularly Reformed Protestants, that they have been enemies of the arts. Critics point out that the Reformers removed religious art from their churches and whitewashed their walls. Lord Harewood, artistic director of Edinburgh Festival, complained in 1963, 'My greatest enemy is still that old Presbyterian, John Knox'.[73] A more accurate assessment, however, would be to see Protestantism as the great liberator of art. Yes, the Reformation tended to restrict the use of visual and musical art forms in worship. Yet, because the Reformation tore down the wall separating the sacred from the secular, it opened a door for artists heretofore closed to non-religious themes. Art, in its proper sphere, was seen as a gift of God and was given positive encouragement. The Reformation liberated art by 'releasing art from the guardianship of the church',[74] said Abraham Kuyper (1837–1920), the great Dutch

2004) attributes almost all the characteristics of the 'American Creed', as he calls it, to the nation's Protestant-dominated founding, heritage and history. He specifies the Protestant virtues as individual conscience, equality, private property, freedom of religion, assembly, speech and the press, the work ethic, moral rectitude, thrift, personal initiative, representative democracy, the rule of law, the responsibility of rulers, and a national mission to serve God: 'Almost all the central ideas of the Creed have their origins in dissenting Protestantism' (p. 68).

[73] J. D. Douglas, 'Calvinism's Contribution to Scotland' in Stanford Reid (ed), *John Calvin*, p. 236.

[74] Kuyper, *Lectures on Calvinism*, p. 157. See evaluation in Peter S. Heslam, *Creating a Christian Worldview: Abraham Kuyper's Lectures on Calvinism* (Grand Rapids: Eerdmans, 1998). For a stimulating discussion of a Protestant worldview and art see H. R. Rookmaaker, *Modern Art & the Death of a Culture* (Downers Grove: Inter-Varsity Press, 1970); Also, G. E. Veith, *State of the Arts: From Bezalel to Mapplethorpe* (Wheaton, Illinois: Crossway Books, 1991).

Calvinist theologian, educator, journalist and politician of the late nineteenth and early twentieth-centuries. 'Calvinism', says Kuyper, 'actually and in a concrete way advanced the development of the arts.'[75] Landscapes, seascapes, still-lives burst on to the scene wherever the Reformation's influence was felt. Nature, as well as grace, was deemed a subject suitable for the artist's consideration. As Francis Schaeffer (1912–84) said of the Reformed Protestant view, 'If God made the flowers, they are worth painting and writing about'.[76] The Reformation's elevation of the ordinary meant that the artist could look for inspiration 'in what is common and of everyday occurrence', continues Kuyper.[77] Because 'ecclesiastical power no longer restrained the artist', the Reformation 'disclosed to art an entirely new world', a world that includes 'the small and insignificant'.[78]

The Reformation's appreciation of the arts included music. Emile Doumergue (1844–1937), the great French biographer of Calvin, asks and answers his own question: 'What did Calvin do for art? Calvin made the Psalter.'[79] In 1562 the completed *Genevan Psalter* was published, with all 150 Psalms in rhyme and metre, most with a distinctive tune. Louis Benson, the outstanding Presbyterian hymnologist of the early twentieth-century said 'It was the conception of one man's [Calvin's] mind and the enterprise of one man's will . . . it was the element . . . for which he found least sympathy among his colleagues and least preparation among the people'.[80] Here too, says Kuyper, the Reformation 'bridled the

---

[75] Ibid., p. 163.

[76] Francis A. Schaeffer, *Art and the Bible* (Downers Grove, Ill.: Inter-Varsity Press, 1973). Sociologist Charles Taylor said of Puritans and Calvinists in his massive study, *Sources of the Self: The Making of Modern Identity*, they 'generated one of the central ideas of modern culture . . . the affirmation of ordinary life' (p. 227; cited in Marshall, *A Kind of Life*, p. 102).

[77] Ibid., p. 166.   [78] Ibid., p. 167.

[79] Emile Doumergue, 'Music in the Work of Calvin', *Banner of Truth*, Vol. 161 (1977), p. 7.

[80] Louis F. Benson, 'John Calvin and the Psalmody of the Reformed Churches', in *Journal of the Presbyterian Historical Society* (Vol. V, Nos. 1–3, Mar–Sept, 1909), p. 4.

tutelage of the church' and music was 'emancipated by it, and the way opened to its splendid modern development'.[81] Louis Bourgeois (1510–61) was invited by Calvin to Geneva and, with Calvin's encouragement, simplified the music of the church so that the people might sing. He introduced the use of rhythm. He exchanged the eight Gregorian modes for the major and minor keys of popular music, and thus 'gave birth to modern tonality'.[82] He adopted the use of harmony, or singing in parts. He 'wedded melody to verse by what is called expression',[83] (that is, singing one syllable per note) says Kuyper. He reduced the number of chords, and gave the lead part to the soprano.

The arts were liberated, not suppressed, by the Reformation. Artistic accomplishments in those lands most influenced by the Reformation are impressive.

In the realm of music, it includes the *French Psalter*, the German chorale, and the incomparable genius of J. S. Bach and his many successors.

In the realm of visual art, it includes the paintings of Rembrandt (1609–69) and the Dutch Masters, and later, of Van Gogh (1853–90).

In the realm of architecture, it includes the church designs of Sir Christopher Wren (such as St Paul's Cathedral) and the simple, plain beauty of the New England Meeting House.

In the realm of English literature, it includes the poetry of John Milton (1608–74) and the prose of John Bunyan, two representatives of English Puritanism.

The Reformation, in its zeal to pursue the glory of God in all of life, had much to do with giving to the world its modern form. By breaking down the wall separating the sacred from the secular it introduced the reforms that would improve the common lot of humanity: a church that understands and respects its own sphere, but which through influence and proclamation of the truth reforms all the other spheres to the glory of God. As we have seen, the influence of the Reformers in other spheres has been

[81] Kuyper, p. 168.   [82] Doumergue, p. 16.   [83] Kuyper, p. 168.

considerable: in politics – democratic republics; in economics – free markets; in education – universal literacy and scientific exploration; in society – strong families and dignity in ordinary labour; in the arts – emancipation from the church and the encouragement of non-religious, common and popular themes in music and visual art.

Kuyper's conviction a hundred years ago was that only Reformed Protestantism had a world-view that was comprehensive and coherent enough to combat and defeat the militant anti-Christian secularism of the modern world. Protestantism's authoritative and infallible Scripture provides the epistemological and ethical foundation to build the church and society. The gospel of faith alone in Christ alone by grace alone answers the fundamental questions of life and satisfies the deepest longings of the human soul. The Bible's understanding of man's chief end – the glory of God – provides a purpose in life beyond the self and the temporal in a way that the modern Epicurean philosophies of self indulgence never can. What is needed is a new generation of Christian preachers, ethicists, politicians, economists, educators, artists, musicians and parents to carry the Christian world-view into their realms of endeavour, aiming to see those realms more, rather than less, conforming to the will of Christ, and more, rather than less, pleasing to God. It falls to us today, who are the heirs of the Reformation world-view, to pursue the glory of God in every sphere of life, until, in Kuyper's words, 'God's holy ordinances shall be established again in the home, in the school, and in the state for the good of the people . . . until the nation pays homage again to God'.[84]

---

[84] Kuyper, p. iii.

Appendix:

PROTESTANT CONFESSIONAL
DOCUMENTS ON JUSTIFICATION

1. THE AUGSBURG CONFESSION, *Articles IV & VI*, 1530 (Lutheran)[1]

Article IV

Also they teach that men can not be justified [obtain forgiveness of sins and righteousness] before God by their own powers, merits, or works; but are justified freely [of grace] for Christ's sake through faith, when they believe that they are received into favour, and their sins forgiven for Christ's sake, who by his death hath satisfied for our sins. This faith doth God impute for righteousness before him (*Rom. 3* and 4).

Article VI

Also they teach that this faith should bring forth good fruits, and that men ought to do the good works commanded of God, because it is God's will, and not on any confidence of meriting justification before God by their works.

For remission of sins and justification is apprehended by faith, as also the voice of Christ witnesseth: 'When ye have done all these things, say, "We are unprofitable servants."'

[1] These confessional statements can be found in Philip Schaff, *The Creeds of Christendom*, Grand Rapids: Baker, revised edition, 1984.

The same also do the ancient writers of the Church teach; for Ambrose saith: 'This is ordained of God, that he that believeth in Christ shall be saved, without works, by faith alone, freely receiving remission of sins.'

2. The Formula of Concord, *Article III, Affirmations and Denials*, 1577 (Lutheran)

Article III
Of the Righteousness of Faith before God

Statement of the Controversy

By unanimous consent (according to the rule of the divine Word and the judgment of the Augsburg Confession), it is taught in our churches that we most wretched sinners are justified before God and saved alone by faith in Christ, so that Christ alone is our righteousness. Now this Jesus Christ, our Saviour and our righteousness, is true God and true man; for the divine and human natures in him are personally united (*Jer.* 23:6; *1 Cor.* 1:30; *2 Cor.* 5:21). It has therefore been asked: According to which nature is Christ our righteousness? And by occasion of this, two errors, and these contrary the one to the other, have disturbed certain churches.

For one part has held that Christ is our righteousness only according to the divine nature, if, that is, he dwell by faith in us; for that all the sins of men, compared with that Godhead thus indwelling by faith, are like one drop of water compared with the broad sea. Against this opinion others, indeed, have asserted that Christ is our righteousness before God, only according to his human nature.

Affirmations

I. To overthrow both errors we unanimously believe, teach, and confess that Christ is truly our righteousness, but yet neither according to the divine nature alone, nor according to the human nature alone, but the whole Christ according to both natures, to wit: in his sole, most absolute obedience which he rendered to the Father even unto death, as God and man, and thereby merited for us the remission of all our sins and eternal life. As it is written: 'As by one man's disobedience many were made sinners, so by the obedience of one shall many be made righteous' (*Rom.* 5:19).

II. We believe, therefore, teach, and confess that this very thing is our righteousness before God, namely, that God remits to us our sins of mere grace, without any respect of our works, going before, present, or following, or of our worthiness or merit. For he bestows and imputes to us the righteousness of the obedience of Christ; for the sake of that righteousness we are received by God into favour and accounted righteous.

III. We believe, also, teach, and confess that faith alone is the means and instrument whereby we lay hold on Christ the Saviour, and so in Christ lay hold on that righteousness which is able to stand before the judgment of God; for that faith, for Christ's sake, is imputed to us for righteousness (*Rom.* 4:5).

IV. We believe, moreover, teach, and confess that this justifying faith is not a bare knowledge of the history of Christ, but such and so great a gift of God as that by it we rightly recognize Christ our Redeemer in the word of the gospel, and confide in him: to wit, that for his obedience' sake alone we have by grace the remission of sins, are accounted holy and righteousness before God the Father, and attain eternal salvation.

V. We believe, teach, and confess that the word justify in this article, conformably to the usage of Holy Scripture, signifies the same as to absolve from sin, as may be understood by the word of Solomon (*Prov.* 17:15): 'He that justifieth the wicked, and he that condemneth the just, even they both are abomination to the LORD.' Also (*Rom.* 8:33): 'Who shall lay anything to the charge of God's elect? It is God that justifieth.'

And if at any time for the word Justification the words Regeneration and Vivification are used (as is done in the Apology of the Augsburg Confession), these words are to be taken in the above-stated signification. For elsewhere these words are to be understood of the renewing of man, which is rightly distinguished from the justification of faith.

VI. We believe, teach, and confess, moreover, that, although they that truly believe in Christ and are born again are even to the hour of death obnoxious to many infirmities and stains, yet they ought not to doubt either of the righteousness which is imputed to them through faith or concerning their eternal salvation, but rather are they firmly to be convinced that, for Christ's sake, according to the promise and unshaken word of the gospel, they have God reconciled to them.

VII. We believe, teach, and confess that, for the preserving of the pure doctrine of the righteousness of faith before God, it is necessary that the exclusive particles (by which the apostle Paul separates the merit of Christ utterly from our works, and attributes that glory to Christ alone) should be most diligently retained, as when Paul writes: *'Of grace, freely, without our deserts, without law, without works, not of works.'* All which expressions amount to this: *'By faith in Christ alone are we justified and saved'* (*Eph.* 2:8; *Rom.* 1:17; 3:24; 4:3 sqq.; *Gal.* 3:11; *Heb.*11).

VIII. We believe, teach, and confess that, although antecedent contrition and subsequent new obedience do not appertain to the article of justification before God, yet we are not to imagine any such justifying faith as can exist and abide with a purpose of evil, to wit: of sinning and acting contrary to conscience. But after that man is justified by faith, then that true and living faith works by love (*Gal.* 5:6), and good works always follow justifying faith, and are most certainly found together with it, provided only it be a true and living faith. For true faith is never alone, but hath always charity and hope in its train.

Denials

We repudiate, therefore, and condemn all the false dogmas, which we will now recount:

I. That Christ is our righteousness only according to his divine nature.

II. That Christ is our righteousness only according to his human nature.

III. That in the prophetic and apostolic declarations, which treat of the righteousness of faith, the words *justify* and *to be justified* are not the same as to absolve and be absolved from sins, and to obtain remission of sins, but that we, through love infused by the Holy Ghost, through the virtues and through the works which flow forth from charity, become in very deed righteous before God.

IV. That faith does not have respect to the sole obedience of Christ, but to his divine nature, so far as that dwells and is efficacious in us, so that by that indwelling our sins are covered.

V. That faith is such a confidence in the obedience of Christ as can abide and have a being even in that man who is void of true repentance, and in whom it is not followed by charity, but who contrary to conscience perseveres in sins.

VI. That not God himself dwells, but only the gifts of God dwell in believers.

VII. That faith bestows salvation upon us for the reason that that renewal which consists in love towards God and our neighbour, commences in us through faith.

VIII. That faith in the matter of justification holds, indeed, the first place, but that renewal and charity also appertain to our righteousness before God, so that renewal and charity, indeed, are not the principal cause of our righteousness, but yet that our righteousness before God (if renewal and charity be wanting) is not whole and perfect.

IX. That believers in Christ are righteous and saved before God, both through the imputed righteousness of Christ and through the new obedience which is begun in them, or partly, indeed, through the imputation of the righteousness of Christ, and partly through the new obedience which is begun in them.

X. That the promised grace is appropriated to us by the faith of the heart, and also by the confession of the mouth, and moreover, also, by other virtuous acts.

XI. That faith does not justify without good works, that therefore good works are necessarily required for righteousness, and that independently of their being present man can not be justified.

3. THE HEIDELBERG CATECHISM, *Questions 60–64, 1563* (Continental Reformed)

Question 60:
How art thou righteous before God?

Answer:
Only by true faith in Jesus Christ; that is, although my conscience accuse me that I have grievously sinned against all the commandments of God, and have never kept any of them, and that I am still prone always to all evil, yet God, without any merit of mine, of mere grace, grants and imputes to me the perfect satisfaction, righteousness, and holiness of Christ, as if I had never committed nor had any sin, and had myself accomplished all the

obedience which Christ has fulfilled for me, if only I accept such benefit with a believing heart.

Question 61:
Why sayest thou that thou art righteous only by faith?

Answer:
Not that I am acceptable to God on account of the worthiness of my faith; but because only the satisfaction, righteousness, and holiness of Christ is my righteousness before God, and I can receive the same and make it my own in no other way than by faith only.

Question 62:
But why can not our good works be the whole or part of the righteousness before God?

Answer:
Because the righteousness which can stand before the judgment-seat of God must be perfect throughout, and wholly conformable to the divine law; whereas even our best works in this life are all imperfect and defiled with sin.

Question 63:
How is it that our good works merit nothing, while yet it is God's will to reward them in this life and in that which is to come?

Answer:
The reward comes not of merit but of grace.

Question 64:
But does not this doctrine make men careless and profane?

Answer:
No; for it is impossible that those who are implanted into Christ by true faith should not bring forth fruits of righteousness.

4. THE BELGIC CONFESSION, *Articles XXII–XXIV*, 1561 (Continental Reformed)

Article XXII
Of Our Justification through Faith in Jesus Christ

We believe that, to attain the true knowledge of this great mystery, the Holy Ghost kindleth in our hearts an upright faith, which embraces Jesus Christ with all his merits, appropriates him, and seeks nothing more besides him. For it must needs follow, either that all things which are requisite to our salvation are not in Jesus Christ, or if all things are in him, that then those who possess Jesus Christ through faith have complete salvation in Him. Therefore, for any to assert that Christ is not sufficient, but that something more is required besides him, would be too gross a blasphemy; for hence it would follow that Christ was but half a Saviour. Therefore we justly say with Paul, *that we are justified by faith alone*, or *by faith without works*. However, to speak more clearly, we do not mean that faith itself justifies us, for it is only an instrument with which we embrace Christ our Righteousness. But Jesus Christ, imputing to us all his merits, and so many holy works, which he hath done for us and in our stead, is our Righteousness. And faith is an instrument that keeps us in communion with him in all his benefits, which, when they become ours, are more than sufficient to acquit us of our sins.

Article XXIII
Our Justification Consists in the Forgiveness of Sin and the Imputation of Christ's Righteousness

We believe that our salvation consists in the remission of our sins for Jesus Christ's sake, and that therein our righteousness before God is implied; as David and Paul teach us, declaring this to be the happiness of man, that God imputes righteousness to him without works. And the same Apostle saith, *that we are justified freely by his grace, through the redemption which is in*

Jesus Christ. And therefore we always hold fast this foundation, ascribing all the glory to God, humbling ourselves before him, and acknowledging ourselves to be such as we really are, without presuming to trust in anything in ourselves, or in any merit of ours, relying and resting upon the obedience of Christ crucified alone, which becomes ours when we believe in him. This is sufficient to cover all our iniquities, and to give us confidence in approaching to God; freeing the conscience of fear, terror, and dread, without following the example of our first father, Adam, who, trembling, attempted to cover himself with fig-leaves. And, verily, if we should appear before God, relying on ourselves or on any other creature, though ever so little, we should, alas! be consumed. And therefore every one must pray with David: *O Lord, enter not into judgment with thy servant: for in thy sight shall no man living be justified.*

Article XXIV
Of Man's Sanctification and Good Works

We believe that this true faith, being wrought in man by the hearing of the Word of God and the operation of the Holy Ghost, doth regenerate and make him a new man, causing him to live a new life and freeing him from the bondage of sin. Therefore it is so far from being true, that this justifying faith makes men remiss in a pious and holy life, that on the contrary without it they would never do any thing out of love to God, but only out of self-love or fear of damnation. Therefore it is impossible that this holy faith can be unfruitful in man: for we do not speak of a vain faith, but of such a faith as is called in Scripture *a faith that worketh by love*, which excites man to the practice of those works which God has commanded in his Word. Which works, as they proceed from the good root of faith, are good and acceptable in the sight of God, forasmuch as they are all sanctified by his grace: howbeit they are of no account towards our justification. For it is by faith in Christ that we are justified, even before we do good works, otherwise they could not be good works any more than the fruit of a tree can be good before the tree itself is good.

Therefore we do good works, but not to merit by them (for what can we merit?) – nay, we are beholden to God for the good works we do, and not he to us, *since it is he that worketh in us both to will and to do of his good pleasure.* Let us therefore attend to what is written: *When ye shall have done all those things which are commanded you, say we are unprofitable servants; we have done that which was our duty to do.*

In the mean time we do not deny that God rewards good works, but it is through his grace that he crowns his gifts. Moreover, though we do good works, we do not found our salvation upon them; for we can do no work but what is polluted by our flesh, and also punishable; and although we could perform such works, still the remembrance of one sin is sufficient to make God reject them. Thus, then, we should always be in doubt, tossed to and fro without any certainty, and our poor consciences would be continually vexed if they relied not on the merits of the suffering and death of our Saviour.

5. THE THIRTY-NINE ARTICLES OF THE CHURCH OF ENGLAND, *Articles XI and XII*, 1571

XI. *Of the Justification of Man*

We are accounted righteous before God, only for the merit of our Lord and Saviour Jesus Christ by Faith, and not for our own works or deservings. Wherefore, that we are justified by Faith only is a most wholesome Doctrine, and very full of comfort, as more largely is expressed in the Homily of Justification.

XII. *Of Good Works*

Albeit that Good Works, which are the fruits of Faith, and follow after Justification, can not put away our sins, and endure the severity of God's judgment; yet are they pleasing and acceptable to God in Christ, and do spring out necessarily of a true and lively Faith; insomuch that by them a lively Faith may be as evidently known as a tree discerned by the fruit.

6. THE WESTMINSTER CONFESSION OF FAITH, *Chapters XI, XIII–XVI, 1647* (Presbyterian)

Chapter XI
Of Justification

1. Those whom God effectually calleth he also freely justifieth; not by infusing righteousness into them, but by pardoning their sins, and by accounting and accepting their persons as righteous: not for any thing wrought in them, or done by them, but for Christ's sake alone; nor by imputing faith itself, the act of believing, or any other evangelical obedience to them, as their righteousness; but by imputing the obedience and satisfaction of Christ unto them, they receiving and resting on him and his righteousness by faith; which faith they have not of themselves, it is the gift of God.

2. Faith, thus receiving and resting on Christ and his righteousness, is the alone instrument of justification; yet is it not alone in the person justified, but is ever accompanied with all other saving graces, and is no dead faith, but worketh by love.

3. Christ, by his obedience and death, did fully discharge the debt of all those that are thus justified, and did make a proper, real, and full satisfaction to his Father's justice in their behalf. Yet inasmuch as he was given by the Father for them, and his obedience and satisfaction accepted in their stead, and both freely, not for any thing in them, their justification is only of free grace; that both the exact justice and rich grace of God might be glorified in the justification of sinners.

4. God did, from all eternity, decree to justify all the elect, and Christ did, in the fullness of time, die for their sins, and rise again for their justification; nevertheless, they are not justified until the Holy Spirit doth, in due time, actually apply Christ unto them.

5. God doth continue to forgive the sins of those that are justified; and although they can never fall from the state of justification, yet they may by their sins fall under God's fatherly displeasure, and not have the light of His countenance restored unto them, until they humble themselves, confess their sins, beg pardon, and renew their faith and repentance.

6. The justification of believers under the Old Testament was, in all these respects, one and the same with the justification of believers under the New Testament.

Chapter XIII
Of Sanctification

1. They, who are once effectually called, and regenerated, having a new heart, and a new spirit created in them, are further sanctified, really and personally, through the virtue of Christ's death and resurrection, by His Word and Spirit dwelling in them: the dominion of the whole body of sin is destroyed, and the several lusts thereof are more and more weakened and mortified; and they more and more quickened and strengthened in all saving graces, to the practice of true holiness, without which no man shall see the Lord.

2. This sanctification is throughout, in the whole man; yet imperfect in this life, there abiding still some remnants of corruption in every part; whence arises a continual and irreconcilable war, the flesh lusting against the Spirit, and the Spirit against the flesh.

3. In which war, although the remaining corruption, for a time, may much prevail; yet, through the continual supply of strength from the sanctifying Spirit of Christ, the regenerate part does

overcome; and so, the saints grow in grace, perfecting holiness in the fear of God.

Chapter XIV
Of Saving Faith

1. The grace of faith, whereby the elect are enabled to believe to the saving of their souls, is the work of the Spirit of Christ in their hearts, and is ordinarily wrought by the ministry of the Word, by which also, and by the administration of the sacraments, and prayer, it is increased and strengthened.

2. By this faith, a Christian believes to be true whatsoever is revealed in the Word, for the authority of God Himself speaking therein; and acts differently upon that which each particular passage thereof contains; yielding obedience to the commands, trembling at the threatenings, and embracing the promises of God for this life, and that which is to come. But the principal acts of saving faith are accepting, receiving, and resting upon Christ alone for justification, sanctification, and eternal life, by virtue of the covenant of grace.

3. This faith is different in degrees, weak or strong; may be often and many ways assailed, and weakened, but gets the victory: growing up in many to the attainment of a full assurance, through Christ, who is both the author and finisher of our faith.

Chapter XV
Of Repentance unto Life

1. Repentance unto life is an evangelical grace, the doctrine whereof is to be preached by every minister of the gospel, as well as that of faith in Christ.

2. By it, a sinner, out of the sight and sense not only of the danger, but also of the filthiness and odiousness of his sins, as contrary to the holy nature, and righteous law of God; and upon

the apprehension of His mercy in Christ to such as are penitent, so grieves for, and hates his sins, as to turn from them all unto God, purposing and endeavouring to walk with Him in all the ways of His commandments.

3. Although repentance is not to be rested in, as any satisfaction for sin, or any cause of the pardon thereof, which is the act of God's free grace in Christ, yet it is of such necessity to all sinners, that none may expect pardon without it.

4. As there is no sin so small, but it deserves damnation; so there is no sin so great, that it can bring damnation upon those who truly repent.

5. Men ought not to content themselves with a general repentance, but it is every man's duty to endeavour to repent of his particular sins, particularly.

6. As every man is bound to make private confession of his sins to God, praying for the pardon thereof; upon which, and the forsaking of them, he shall find mercy; so, he that scandalizes his brother, or the Church of Christ, ought to be willing, by a private or public confession, and sorrow for his sin, to declare his repentance to those that are offended, who are thereupon to be reconciled to him, and in love to receive him.

Chapter XVI
Of Good Works

1. Good works are only such as God has commanded in His holy Word, and not such as, without the warrant thereof, are devised by men, out of blind zeal, or upon any pretence of good intention.

2. These good works, done in obedience to God's commandments, are the fruits and evidences of a true and lively faith: and by them believers manifest their thankfulness, strengthen their assurance, edify their brethren, adorn the profession of the gospel,

stop the mouths of the adversaries, and glorify God, whose workmanship they are, created in Christ Jesus thereunto, that, having their fruit unto holiness, they may have the end, eternal life.

3. Their ability to do good works is not at all of themselves, but wholly from the Spirit of Christ. And that they may be enabled thereunto, beside the graces they have already received, there is required an actual influence of the same Holy Spirit, to work in them to will, and to do, of His good pleasure: yet are they not hereupon to grow negligent, as if they were not bound to perform any duty unless upon a special motion of the Spirit; but they ought to be diligent in stirring up the grace of God that is in them.

4. They who, in their obedience, attain to the greatest height which is possible in this life, are so far from being able to super-erogate, and to do more than God requires, as that they fall short of much which in duty they are bound to do.

5. We cannot by our best works merit pardon of sin, or eternal life at the hand of God, by reason of the great disproportion that is between them and the glory to come; and the infinite distance that is between us and God, whom, by them, we can neither profit, nor satisfy for the debt of our former sins, but when we have done all we can, we have done but our duty, and are unprofitable servants: and because, as they are good, they proceed from His Spirit, and as they are wrought by us, they are defiled, and mixed with so much weakness and imperfection, that they cannot endure the severity of God's judgment.

6. Notwithstanding, the persons of believers being accepted through Christ, their good works also are accepted in Him; not as though they were in this life wholly unblameable and unreproveable in God's sight; but that He, looking upon them in His Son, is pleased to accept and reward that which is sincere, although accompanied with many weaknesses and imperfections.

7. Works done by unregenerate men, although for the matter of them they may be things which God commands; and of good use both to themselves and others: yet, because they proceed not from an heart purified by faith; nor are done in a right manner, according to the Word; nor to a right end, the glory of God, they are therefore sinful and cannot please God, or make a man meet to receive grace from God: and yet, their neglect of them is more sinful and displeasing unto God.

INDEX